THE UKULELE
5 Chord Songbook

PLAY 50 GREAT SONGS WITH JUST 5 EASY CHORDS!

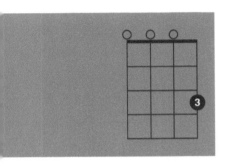

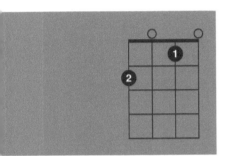

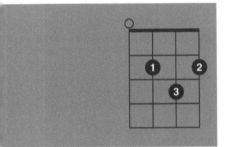

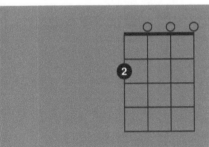

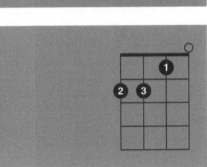

ISBN 978-1-4950-1236-5

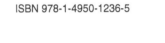
HAL•LEONARD®
CORPORATION

7777 W. BLUEMOUND RD. P.O. BOX 13819 MILWAUKEE, WI 53213

Visit Hal Leonard Online at
www.halleonard.com

5 Chord Songbook

PLAY 50 GREAT SONGS WITH JUST 5 EASY CHORDS!

Contents

Another Day in Paradise

Words and Music by Phil Collins

First note

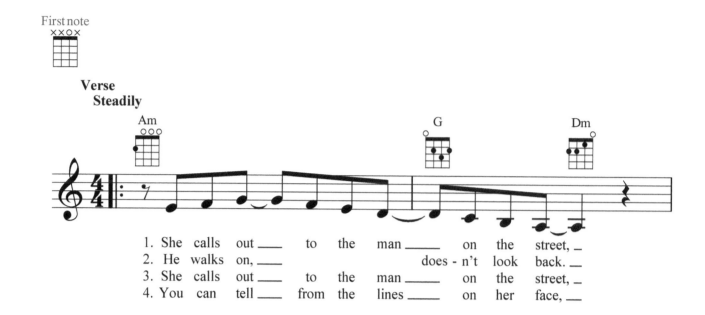

Verse
Steadily

1. She calls out ___ to the man ___ on the street, ___
2. He walks on, ___   does - n't look back. ___
3. She calls out ___ to the man ___ on the street, ___
4. You can tell ___ from the lines ___ on her face, ___

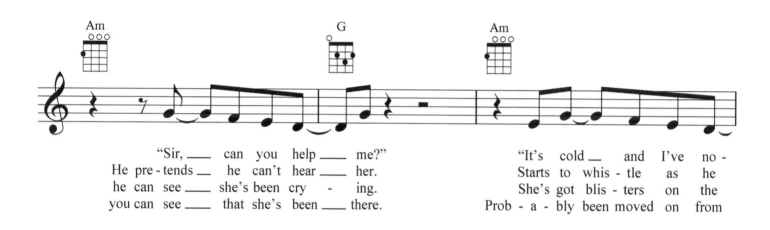

"Sir, ___ can you help ___ me?"   "It's cold ___ and I've no -
He pre - tends ___ he can't hear ___ her.   Starts to whis - tle as he
he can see ___ she's been cry - ing.   She's got blis - ters on the
you can see ___ that she's been ___ there.   Prob - a - bly been moved on from

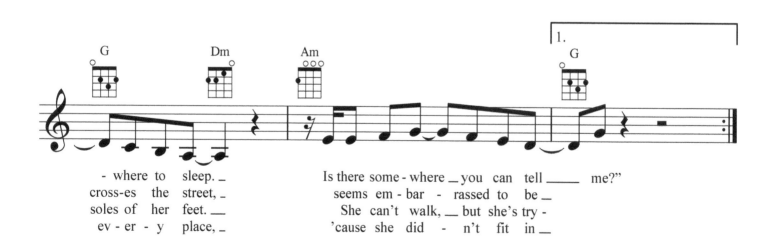

1.

- where to sleep. ___   Is there some - where ___ you can tell ___ me?"
cross - es the street, ___   seems em - bar - rassed to be ___
soles of her feet. ___   She can't walk, ___ but she's try -
ev - er - y place, ___   'cause she did - n't fit in ___

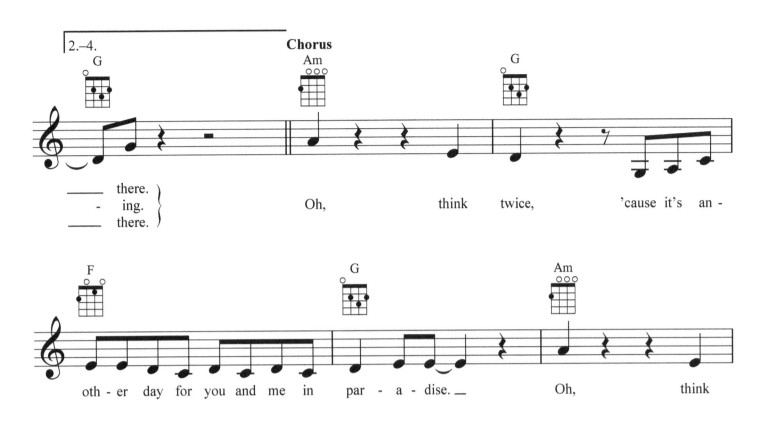

2.–4.

Chorus

there.
- ing.
there.

Oh, think twice, 'cause it's an -

oth - er day for you and me in par - a - dise. __ Oh, think

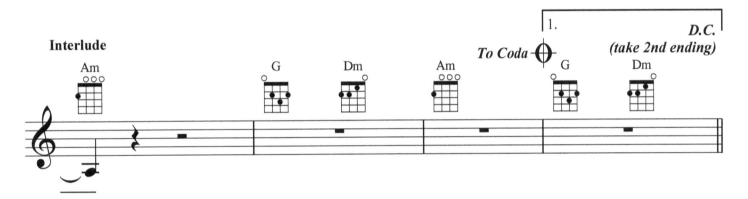

twice, 'cause it's an - oth - er day for you, __ you and me in par - a - dise. __

Interlude

To Coda ⊕

1.

D.C.
(take 2nd ending)

2.

Bridge

Oh, Lord, __ is there

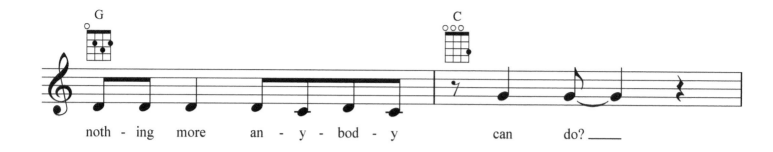

noth - ing more an - y - bod - y can do? ____

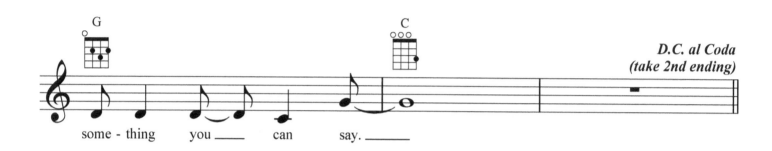

Oh, _____ Lord, ____ there must be

D.C. al Coda
(take 2nd ending)

some - thing you ____ can say. ____

⊕ Coda

Outro

It's just an - oth - er day ____ for

Repeat and fade

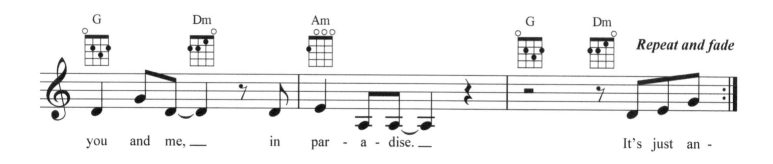

you and me, ____ in par - a - dise. ____ It's just an -

Breakeven

Words and Music by Stephen Kipner, Andrew Frampton, Daniel O'Donoghue and Mark Sheehan

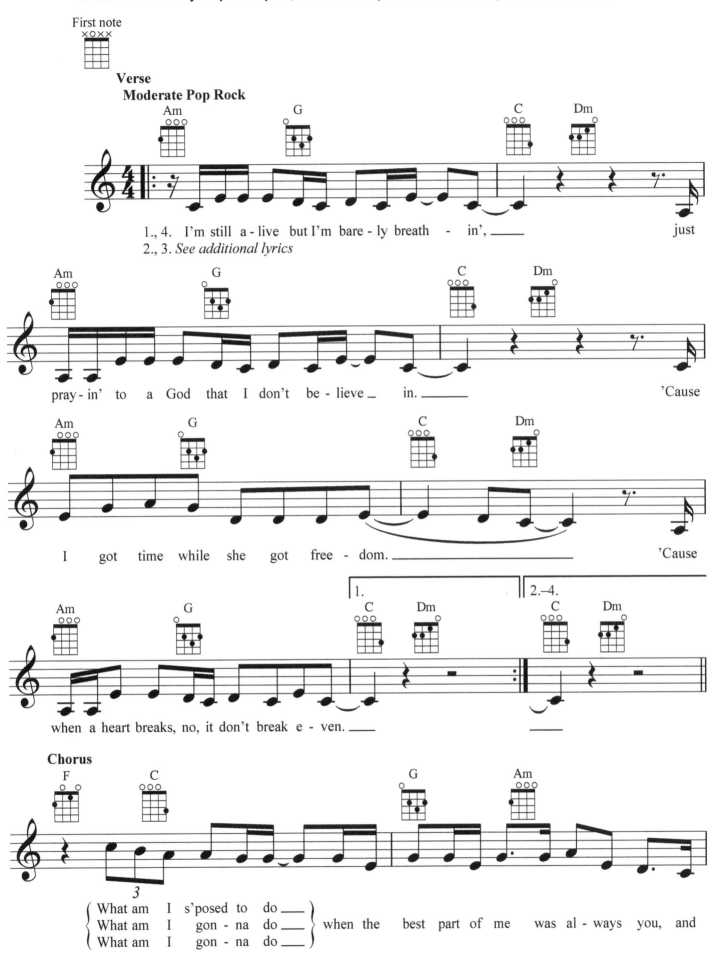

what am I s'posed to say ___ when I'm all choked up that you're _ o - kay? ___

I'm fall - in' to piec - es, ___ yeah, ___ I'm fall - in' to piec -

- es. ___ 3. They

Coda 1

Interlude

- es. ___

Bridge

Oh, ___ you got his heart and my heart and none of the pain.

You took your suit-case; I took the blame. Now I'm tryin' to make sense of what lit-tle re-mains, ___

Additional Lyrics

2. Her best days will be some of my worst.
   She finally met a man that's gonna put her first.
   While I'm wide awake, she's no trouble sleepin',
   'Cause when a heart breaks, no, it don't break even.

3. They say bad things happen for a reason,
   But no wise word's gonna stop the bleedin'.
   'Cause she's moved on while I'm still grievin',
   And when a heart breaks, no, it don't break even.

Baby Can I Hold You

Words and Music by Tracy Chapman

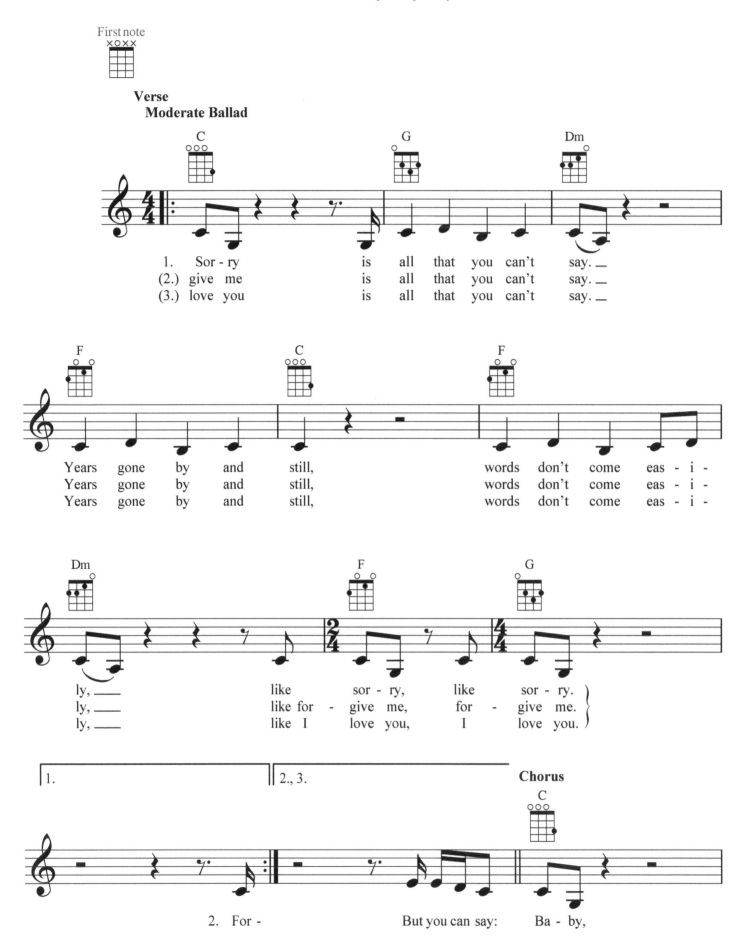

ba - by, can I hold ___ you to - night? ___

May - be if I told ___ you the right words, ooh, ___ at the right ___

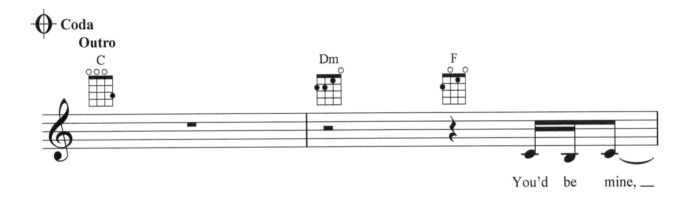

To Coda ⊕

D.C. al Coda
(take 2nd ending)

___ time, you'd be mine. 3. I

⊕ **Coda**
Outro

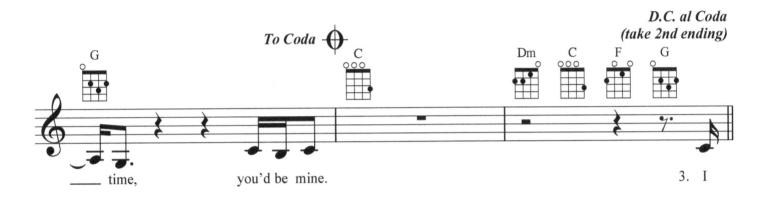

You'd be mine, ___

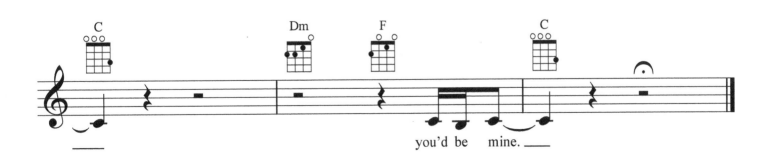

you'd be mine. ___

Come Pick Me Up

Words and Music by Ryan Adams and Van Alston

First note

Verse
Slow Shuffle

1. When they call ___ your name, ___ will you walk ___ right up
2. When you're walk - ing down - town, ___ do you wish I was there?

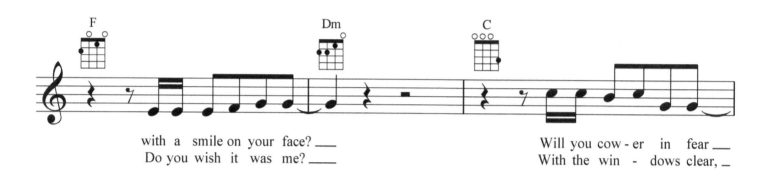

with a smile on your face? ___ Will you cow - er in fear ___
Do you wish it was me? ___ With the win - dows clear, ___

___ in your fa - v'rite sweat-er ___ with an old love let - ter? ___
___ in the man-ne-quins' eyes, ___ do they all look like mine? ___

Pre-Chorus

I wish ___ you ___ would, ___ ⎫   I wish ___ you ___ would ___
You know ___ you ___ could, ___ ⎭

come pick me up, _____ take me out, _____ f**k me up, _

_____ steal my rec-ords, _ { screw all my friends; _ they're all full of sh**... _
{ screw all my friends _ be - hind _ my back... _

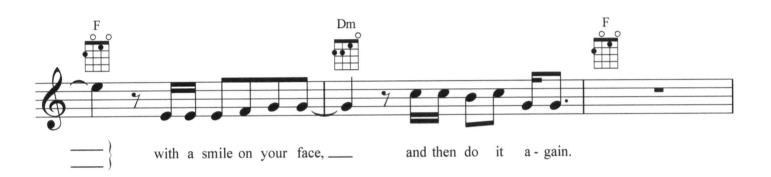

_____ } with a smile on your face, ___ and then do it a - gain.

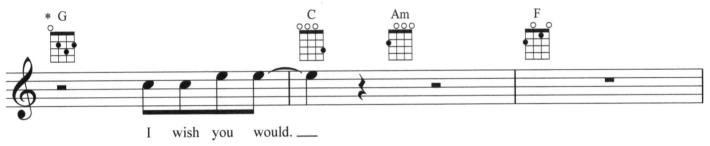

I wish you would. ___

* Let chord ring.

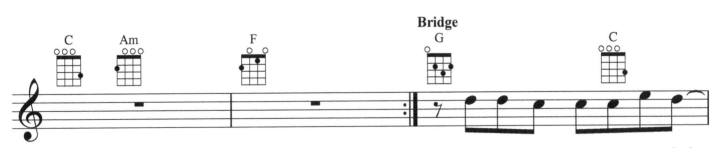

I wish you'd make up my bed _

so   I   could   make   up   my   mind, ___

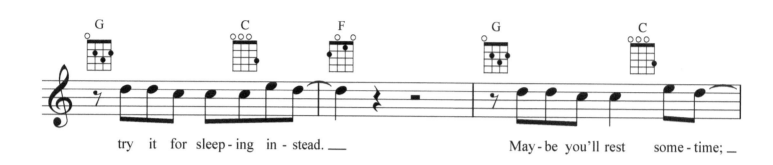

try   it   for   sleep-ing   in-stead. ___   May-be   you'll   rest   some-time; __

Outro

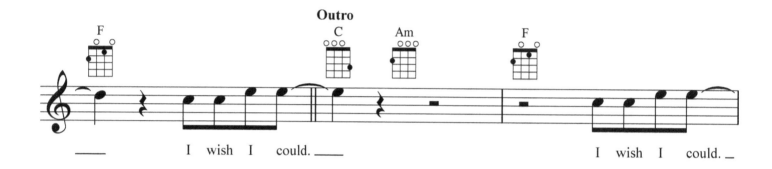

___   I   wish   I   could. ___   I   wish   I   could. __

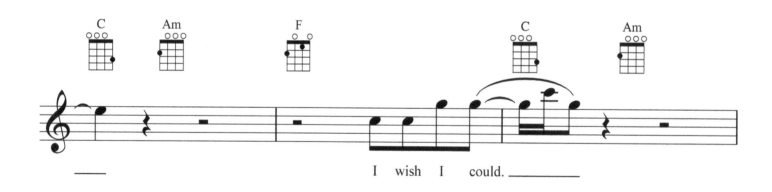

___   I   wish   I   could. ___

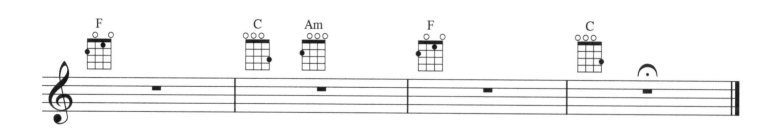

Counting Stars

Words and Music by Ryan Tedder

Verse

Am

life   like a swing-in' vine, _____ swing my heart a-cross the line. __

(2.) *See additional lyrics*

G   **F**

In my face is flash-in' signs, __ seek it out and ye shall find. __ }

Am   **C**

Old,   but I'm not that old.   Young,   but I'm not that bold.   And

G   **F**

I don't think the world is sold __ on just do-in' what we're told. __

Pre-Chorus

Am   **C**   **G**

I,   I _____ feel __ some-thin' so   right   do-in' the wrong __

F   **Am**   **C**

____ thing. _____ And I, I _____ feel __ some-thin' so

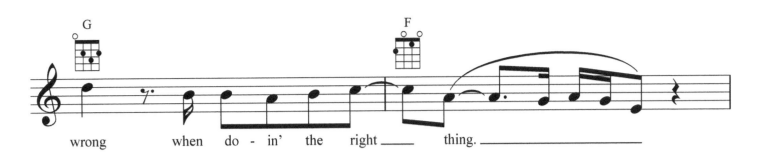

wrong   when   do - in' the   right ____ thing. _____

I could - n't lie, could - n't   lie, could - n't lie. ____   Ev - 'ry - thing _ that
                                                              Ev - 'ry - thing _ that

%𝄋 **Chorus**

N.C.

kills   me   makes me   feel   a - live.   Late - ly   I   been, ____
drowns me   makes me   wan - na   fly.

I   been los - in' sleep ____   dream - in' a - bout ____ the things that

we   could   be.   But,   ba - by,   I   been, _   I been pray - in' hard. _

Said   no more count - in' dol - lars,   we'll be count - in' stars.   Late - ly   I   been, _

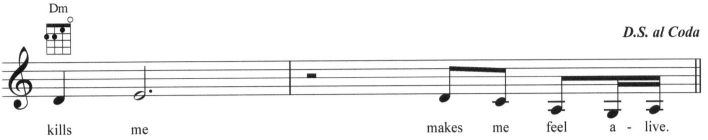

kills me makes me feel a - live.

Coda
Outro-Bridge

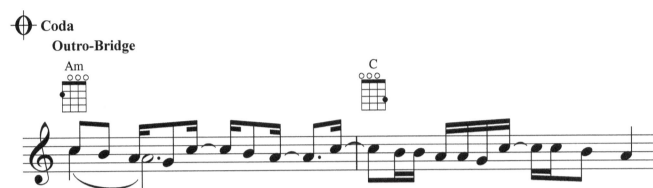

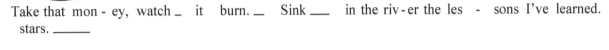

Take that mon-ey, watch __ it burn. __ Sink __ in the riv-er the les - sons I've learned.
stars. _____

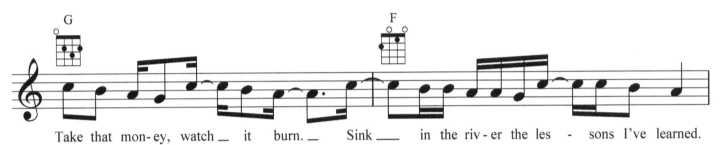

Take that mon-ey, watch __ it burn. __ Sink __ in the riv-er the les - sons I've learned.

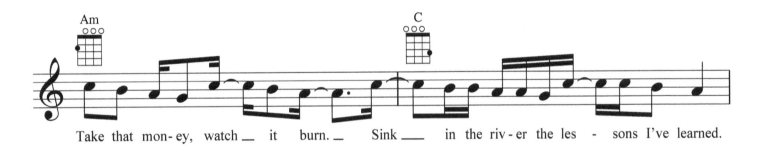

Take that mon-ey, watch __ it burn. __ Sink __ in the riv-er the les - sons I've learned.

Take that mon-ey, watch __ it burn. __ Sink __ in the riv-er the les - sons I've learned.

Additional Lyrics

2. I feel your love, and I feel it burn
Down this river, every turn.
Hope is a four-letter word.
Make that money, watch it burn.

Come to My Window

Words and Music by Melissa Etheridge

First note

Intro
Moderately slow

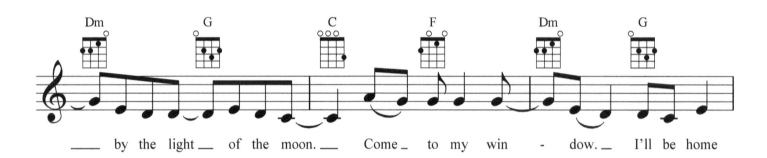

Come to my win - dow. _ Crawl in - side, wait _

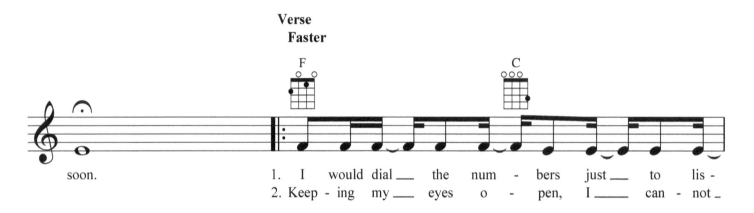

_ by the light _ of the moon. _ Come _ to my win - dow. _ I'll be home

Verse
Faster

soon.

1. I would dial _ the num - bers just _ to lis -
2. Keep - ing my _ eyes o - pen, I _ can - not _

- ten to _ your breath. _ And I would stand _ in - side _ my hell _ and hold _
_ af - ford _ to sleep. _ Giv - ing a - way prom - is - es _ I know _

_____ the hand _ of death. ___   You don't know _ how far ___ I'd go ___ to
_____ that I ___ can't keep. ___   Noth - ing fills ___ the black - ness that ___ has

ease this ___ pre - cious ache. ___   And you don't know _ how much _ I'd give ___ or
seeped in - to my chest. ___   I need you in ___ my blood; _ I am ___ for -

Pre-Chorus

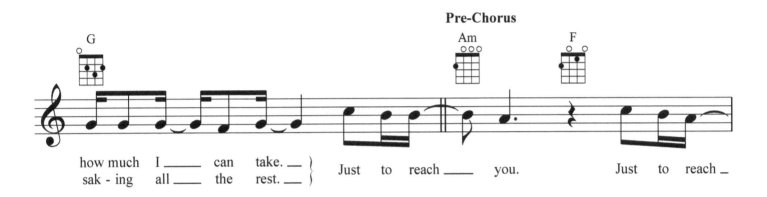

how much I ___ can take. ___ ⎫
sak - ing all ___ the rest. ___ ⎭   Just to reach ___ you.   Just to reach _

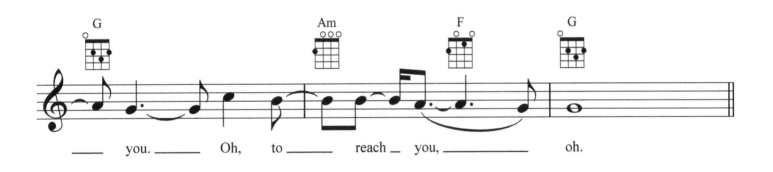

_____ you. _____ Oh, to ___ reach _ you, _____ oh.

Chorus

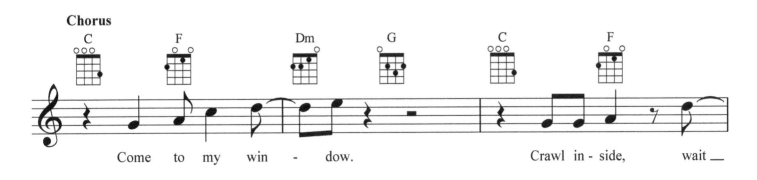

Come to my win - dow.   Crawl in - side, wait _

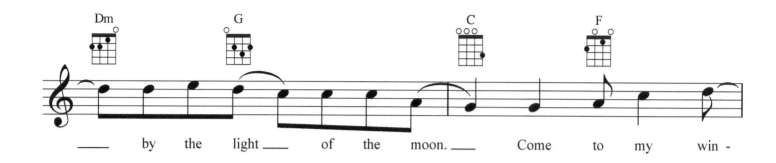

_____ by the light _____ of the moon. _____ Come to my win-

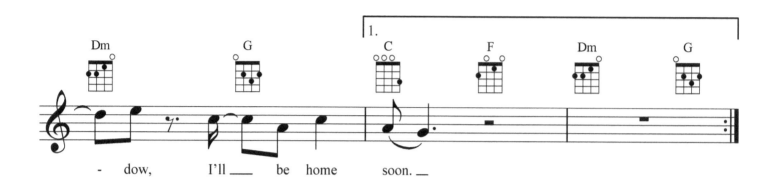

- dow,   I'll _____ be home   soon. _____

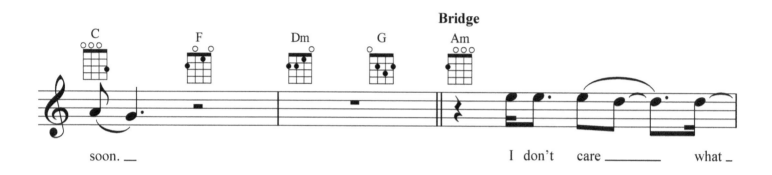

Bridge

soon. _____   I don't care _____ what _

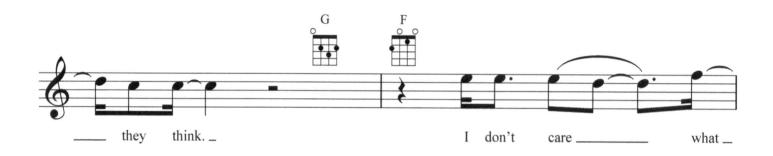

_____ they think. _   I don't care _____ what _

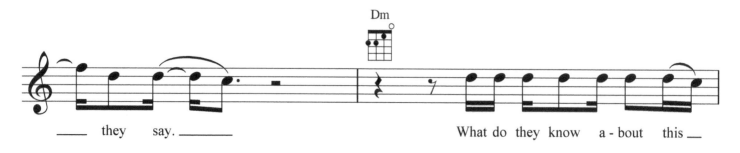

_____ they   say. _____   What do they know a - bout this _

love ___ an - y - way? _____

Outro-Chorus

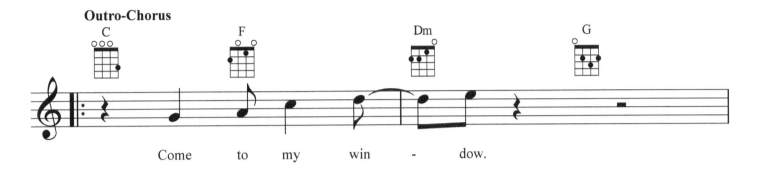

Come to my win - dow.

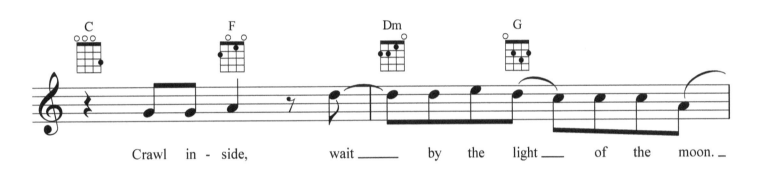

Crawl in - side, wait _____ by the light ___ of the moon. _

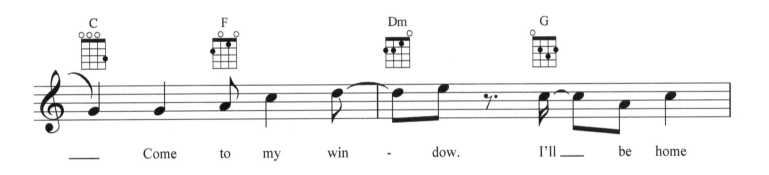

___ Come to my win - dow. I'll ___ be home

Repeat and fade

soon, _____ I'll ___ be home, _ I'll ___ be home. _ I'm com - in' home. _____

Cups
(When I'm Gone)

from the Motion Picture Soundtrack PITCH PERFECT
Words and Music by A.P. Carter, Luisa Gerstein and Heloise Tunstall-Behrens

the one with the pret-ti-est ___ of views. It's got

moun-tains, it's got riv-ers, it's got sights to give you shiv-ers, ___ but it

D.S. al Coda

Coda

sure would be pret-ti-er ___ with you. When I'm

gone. When I'm

Outro-Chorus

gone, when I'm gone, _____ you're gon-na miss ___ me when I'm

gone. You're gon-na miss me by my walk, ___ you're gon-na

miss me by my talk. __ Oh, you're gon-na miss ___ me when I'm gone.

Don't Panic

Words and Music by Guy Berryman, Jon Buckland, Will Champion and Chris Martin

* Optional tab may not match simplified chord diagrams.

We live in a beau - ti - ful world, _____

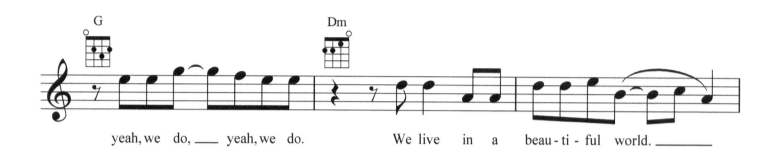

yeah, we do, ___ yeah, we do. We live in a beau - ti - ful world. _____

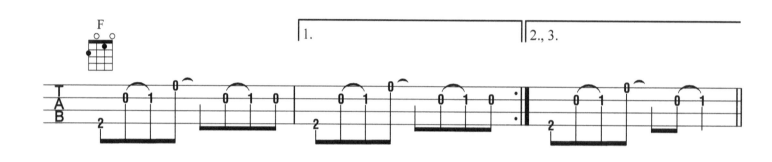

Interlude

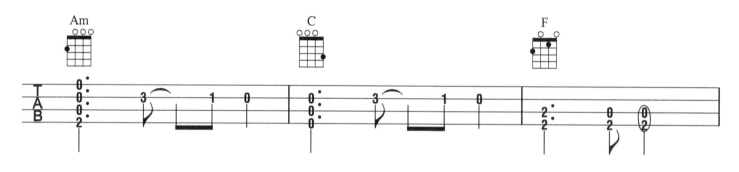

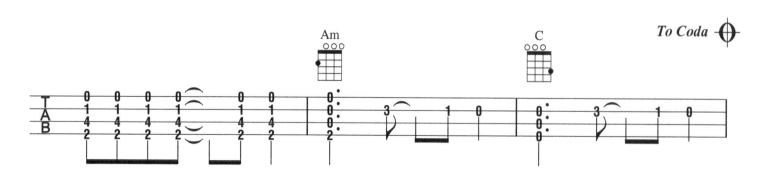

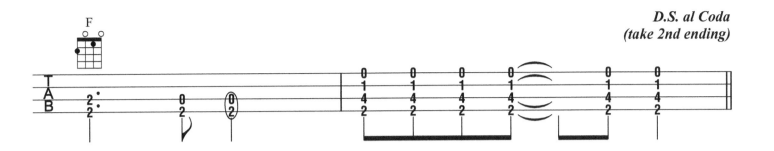

Coda

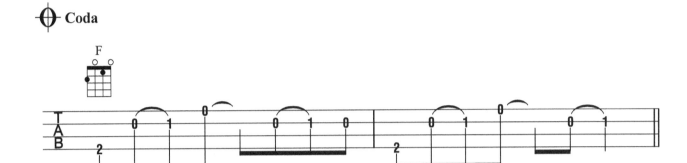

Outro-Verse

Oh, all _____ that I know, there's noth - ing here to

run from. 'Cause, yeah, ev - 'ry - bod - y

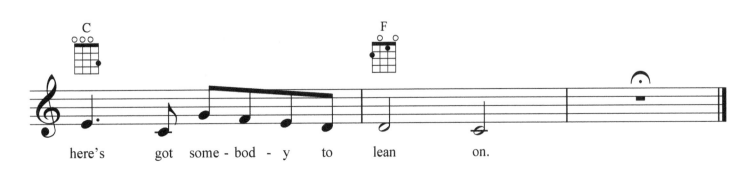

here's got some - bod - y to lean on.

From a Distance

Words and Music by Julie Gold

First note

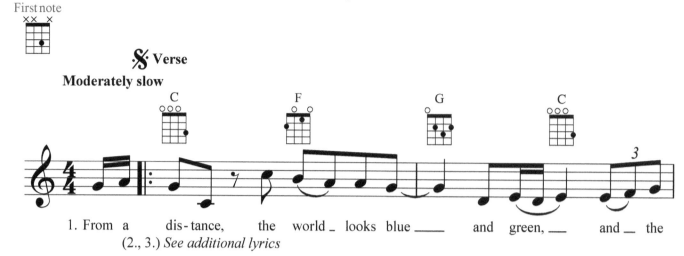

Verse
Moderately slow

1. From a dis-tance, the world ___ looks blue ___ and green, ___ and ___ the
(2., 3.) *See additional lyrics*

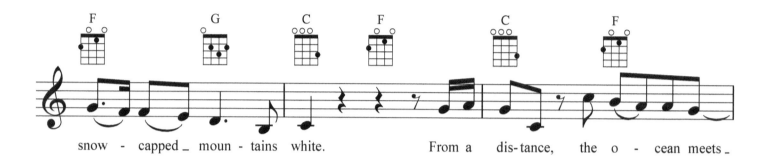

snow - capped ___ moun - tains white. From a dis-tance, the o - cean meets ___

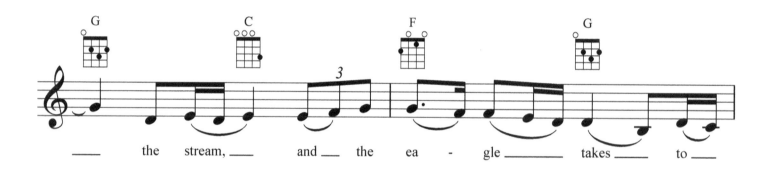

___ the stream, ___ and ___ the ea - gle ___ takes ___ to ___

Chorus

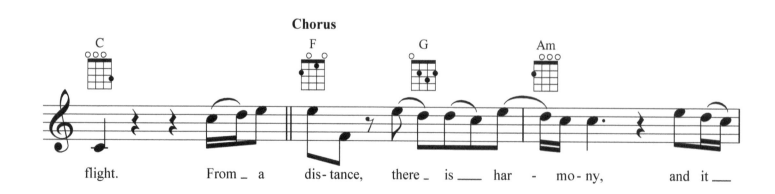

flight. From ___ a dis-tance, there ___ is ___ har - mo - ny, and it ___

Outro-Bridge

song of __ ev - 'ry man. _____ God __ is

watch - ing us, ___ God __ is watch - ing _____ us, God __ is

watch - ing us from a ___ dis - tance. _____ Oh, God __ is

watch - ing us, ___ God __ is watch - ing, _____ God __ is

watch - ing us _____ from a dis - tance.

Let chord ring.

Additional Lyrics

2. From a distance, we all have enough,
   And no one is in need.
   And there are no guns, no bombs and no disease,
   No hungry mouths to feed.

Chorus: From a distance, we are instruments,
   Marching in a common band,
   Playing songs of hope, playing songs of peace.
   They're the songs of ev'ry man.

3. From a distance, you look like my friend,
   Even though we are at war.
   From a distance, I just cannot comprehend
   What all this fighting is for.

Chorus: From a distance, there is harmony,
   And it echoes through the land.
   It's the hope of hopes, it's the love of loves,
   It's the heart of ev'ry man.

For You

Words and Music by John Denver

you a - lone, _____ on - ly for you.

Interlude

3. Just to wake up each you.

rit.

Just the words of a

**Outro-Verse
Slower**

love song, just the beat of my heart,

rit.

just the pledge of my life, my love, for you. _____

Fugitive

Words and Music by Robbie Malone, Keith Prior and David Gray

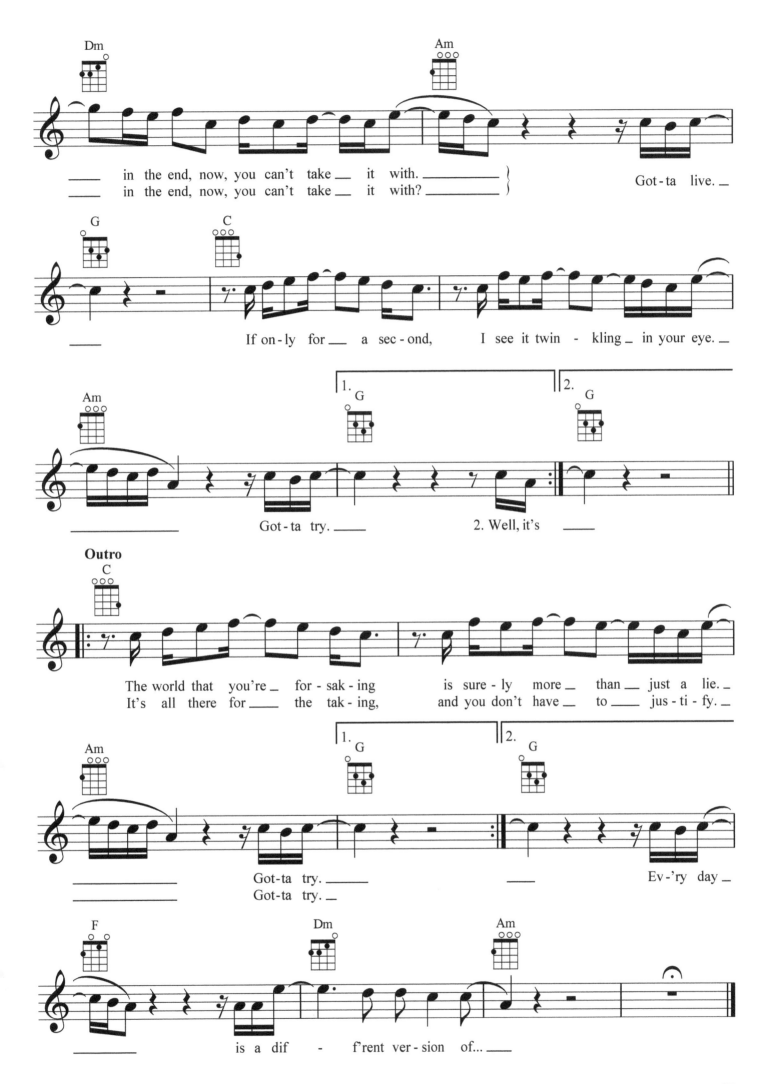

Garden Party

Words and Music by Rick Nelson

they all knew my name, _____ but no one rec - og - nized _____ me; I did - n't look the same. _____ But it's

Chorus

all right now, _____ I learned my les - son well. _ _____ You see, you can't please ev - 'ry - one, _____ so you got to please your - self. _____

To Coda ⊕

1.

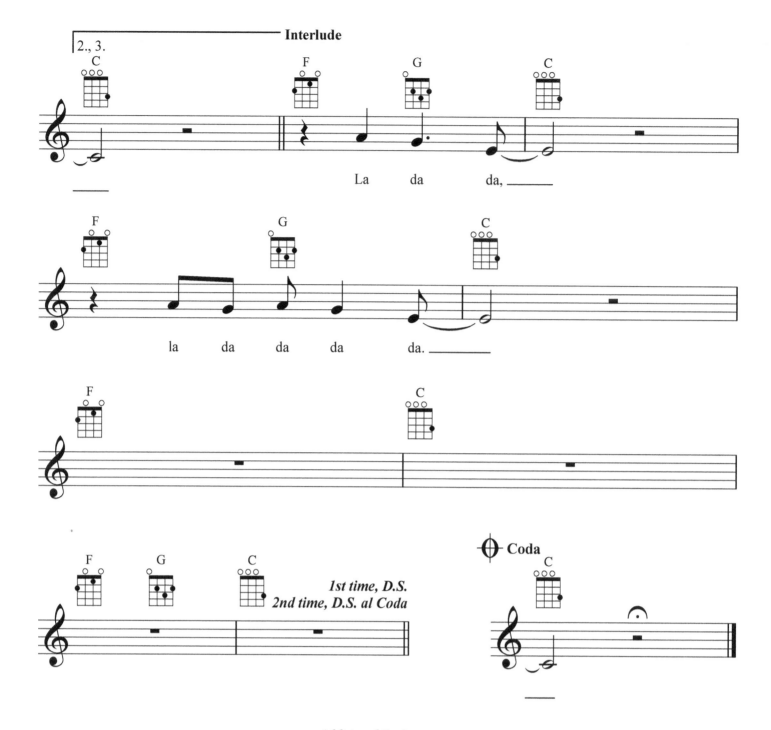

Additional Lyrics

2. People came for miles around; everyone was there.
   Yoko brought her walrus; there was magic in the air.
   And over in the corner, much to my surprise,
   Mr. Hughes hid in Dylan's shoes, wearing his disguise.

3. I played them all the old songs; I thought that's why they came.
   No one heard the music; we didn't look the same.
   I said hello to Mary Lou; she belongs to me.
   When I sang a song about a honky-tonk, it was time to leave.

4. Someone opened up a closet door and out stepped Johnny B. Goode,
   Playing guitar like a-ringin' a bell, and lookin' like he should.
   If you gotta play at garden parties, I wish you a lotta luck;
   But if memories were all I sang, I'd rather drive a truck.

Island in the Sun

Words and Music by Rivers Cuomo

First note

1. When you're on _____ a hol - i - day, ___
2. When you're on _____ a gold - en sea, ___

___ ___ you can't find _____ no words ___ to say ___
___ ___ you don't need _____ no mem - o - ry, ___

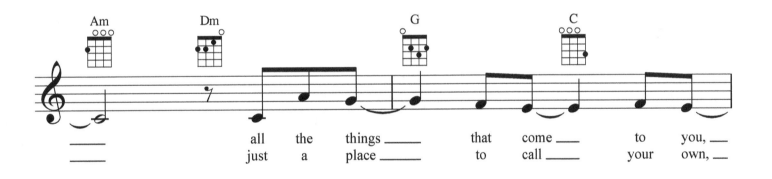

___ all the things _____ that come ___ to you, ___
___ just a place _____ to call _____ your own, ___

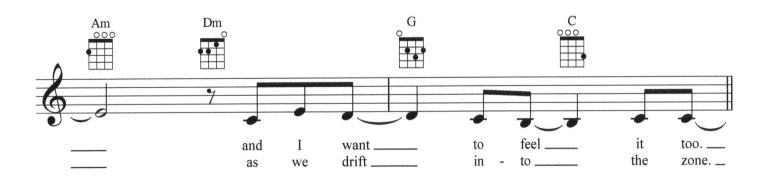

___ and I want _____ to feel ___ it too. ___
___ as we drift _____ in - to _____ the zone. ___

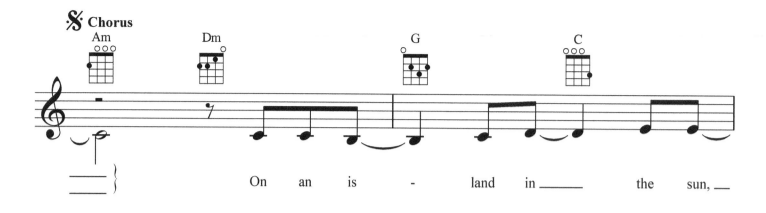

On an is - land in _____ the sun, _____

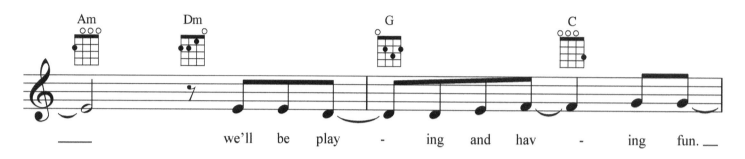

_____ we'll be play - ing and hav - ing fun. _____

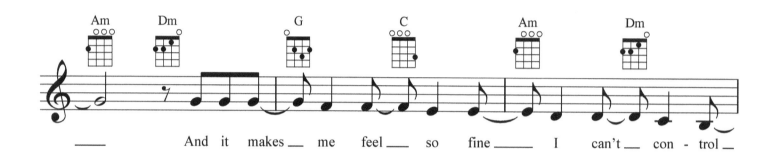

_____ And it makes _ me feel _ so fine _____ I can't _ con - trol _

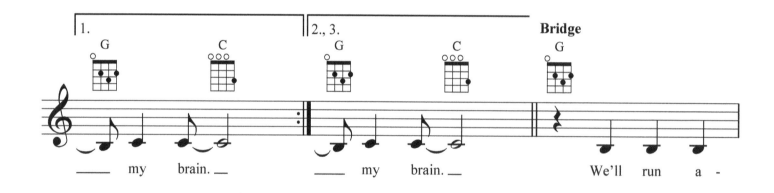

1.
_____ my brain. _

2., 3.
_____ my brain. _

Bridge
We'll run a -

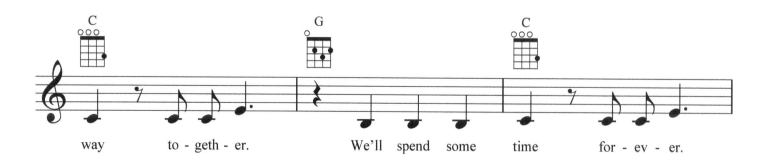

way to - geth - er. We'll spend some time for - ev - er.

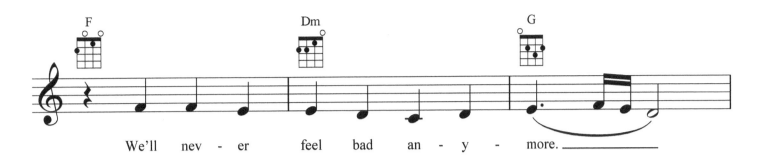

We'll nev - er feel bad an - y - more. _____

Interlude

To Coda ⊕

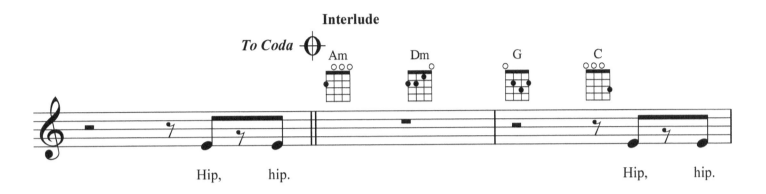

Hip, hip.   Hip, hip.

D.S. al Coda
(take 2nd ending)

Outro

⊕ **Coda**

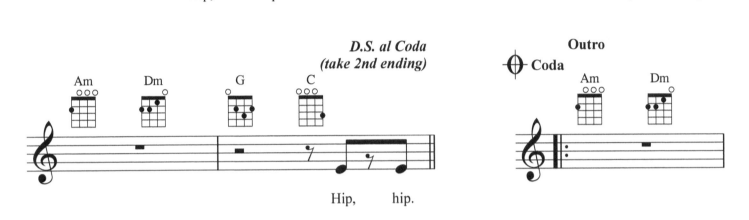

Hip, hip.

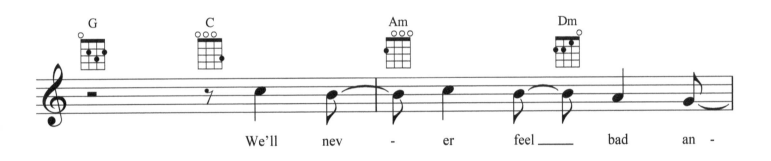

We'll nev - er feel ____ bad an -

Repeat and fade

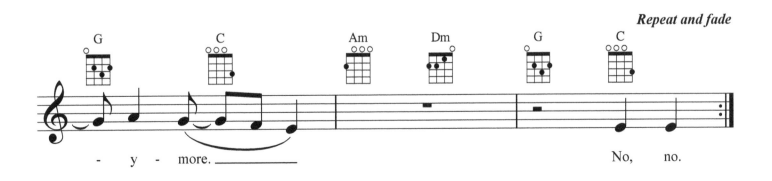

- y - more. _____   No, no.

Gypsy

Words and Music by Stefani Germanotta, Nadir "RedOne" Khayat and Hugo Leclercq

To Coda ⊕

to - night.

Verse

2. So I just packed my

bag - gage ___ and ___ said good-bye ___ to fam - 'ly and friends, ___

and took a road to no - where on my own. _____

Like Dor - 'thy on a yel - low brick, _____

hope my ru - by shoes get us there quick, __ 'cause I left

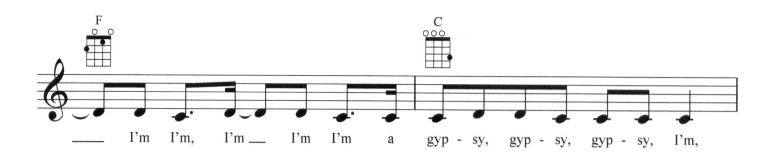

_____ I'm I'm, I'm _____ I'm I'm a gyp - sy, gyp - sy, gyp - sy, I'm,

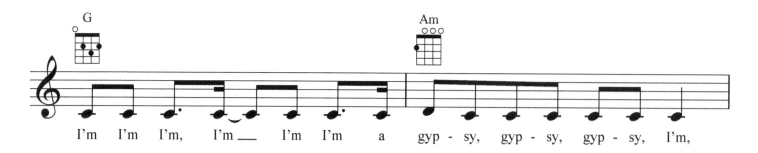

I'm I'm I'm, I'm _____ I'm I'm a gyp - sy, gyp - sy, gyp - sy, I'm,

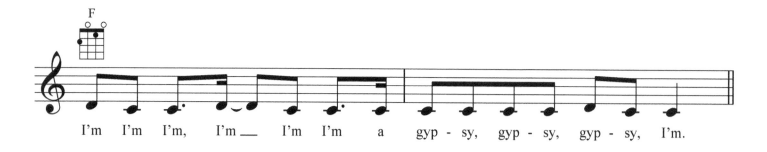

I'm I'm I'm, I'm _____ I'm I'm a gyp - sy, gyp - sy, gyp - sy, I'm.

Bridge 2

And then he asked me, he said, "Ba - by, _____ why _____

_____ do we love each oth - er?" _____

I _____ said, "Hon - ey, it's sim - ple; it's the way _____ that you love _____

Pre-Chorus

and treat your moth - er." ___ Thought that I would be a -

lone for - ev - er, but I won't be to - night. ___

I'm a man with - out a home, but I ___ think, with

you I ___ could spend my ___ life. ___ And you'll be my lit - tle

gyp - sy prin - cess. Pack your bags and we can ___

___ chase the sun - set. ___ Bust the rear - view ___ and

fire up ___ the jets, 'cause ___ it's you and ___ me, _____

N.C.

Outro

G   Am

ba - by,   for life, _____

F   C   G

___   (If you'll go   with   me.) ___   for   life. _____

Am   F   C

(See the world   with   me.) ___   'Cause

G   Am

I'm   I'm   I'm,   I'm ___   I'm   I'm   a   gyp - sy,   gyp - sy,   gyp - sy,   I'm,

F   C

I'm   I'm   I'm,   I'm ___   I'm   I'm   a   gyp - sy,   gyp - sy,   gyp - sy,   I'm

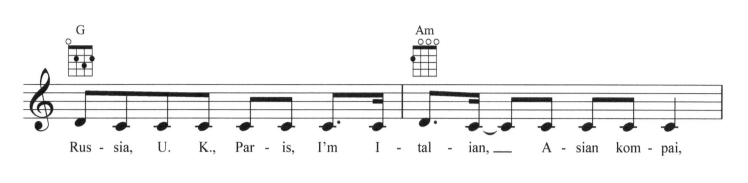

Rus - sia, U. K., Par - is, I'm I - tal - ian, __ A - sian kom - pai,

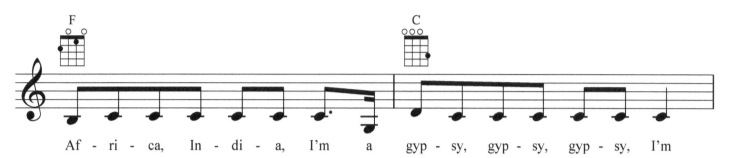

Af - ri - ca, In - di - a, I'm a gyp - sy, gyp - sy, gyp - sy, I'm

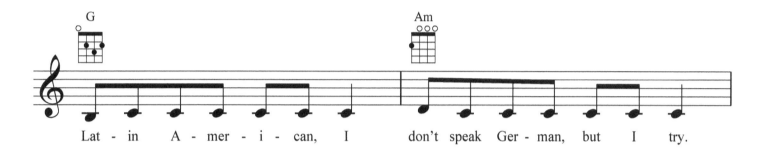

Lat - in A - mer - i - can, I don't speak Ger - man, but I try.

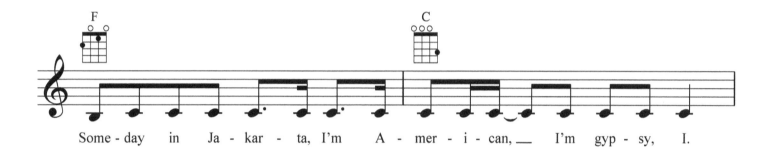

Some - day in Ja - kar - ta, I'm A - mer - i - can, __ I'm gyp - sy, I.

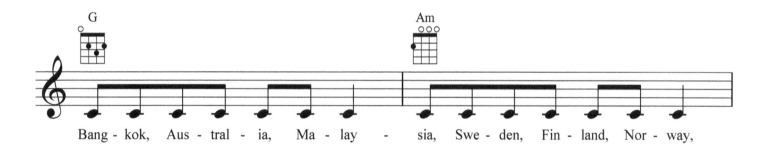

Bang - kok, Aus - tral - ia, Ma - lay - sia, Swe - den, Fin - land, Nor - way,

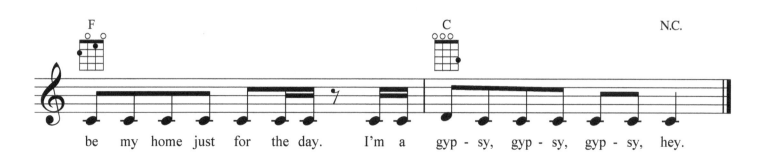

be my home just for the day. I'm a gyp - sy, gyp - sy, gyp - sy, hey.

I Bet My Life

Words and Music by Daniel Reynolds, Daniel Sermon,
Benjamin McKee and Daniel Platzman

I Hope You Dance

Words and Music by Tia Sillers and Mark D. Sanders

First note

Verse
Moderately, in 2

1. I hope you nev - er lose _____ your sense of
(2.) nev - er fear _____ those _____ moun - tains in the

won - der. You get your fill _____ to eat, _____ but al -
dis - tance. Nev - er set - tle for _____ the path _____

- ways keep that hun - ger. May you
_____ of least re - sist - ance. Liv - in'

nev - er take _____ one sin - gle breath _____ for grant - ed.
might mean tak - in' chanc - es if they're worth tak - in'.

God for - bid ____ love ev - er leave ____ you emp - ty - hand -
Lov - in' might ____ be a mis - take, _____ but it's ___ worth mak -

- ed. I hope you still ____ feel small __ when you
- in'. Don't let _____ some hell - bent ___

stand be - side _____ the o - cean. When - ev - er one ___
heart leave _____ you bit - ter. When you come close __

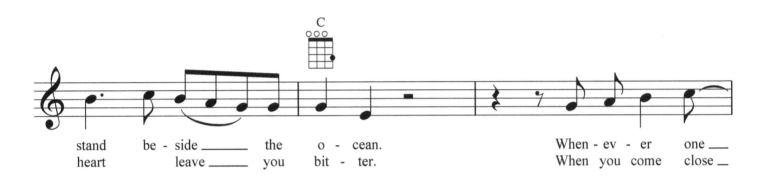

____ door clos - es, I _____ hope one ___ more o - pens.
____ to sell - in' out, _____ re - con - sid - er.

Prom - ise me _____ that you'll __ give faith _____ a fight - ing
Give the heav - ens a - bove more ____ than just a pass - ing

chance.
glance.

And when you get the choice to

To Coda ⊕

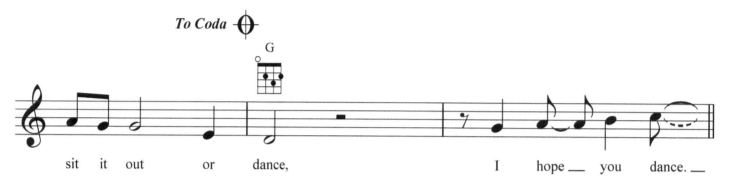

sit it out or dance, I hope ___ you dance. ___

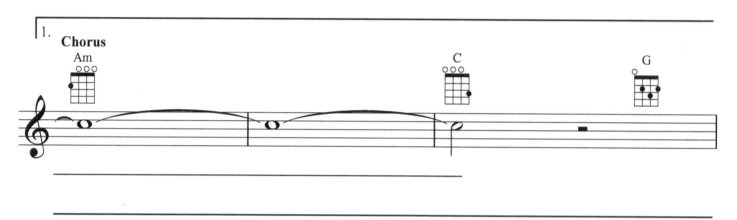

1.

Chorus

Chorus

I hope ___ you dance. _____

2.

Bridge-Chorus

G

2. I hope ___ you _____

(Time is a

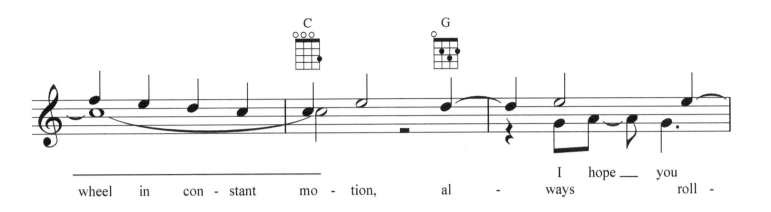

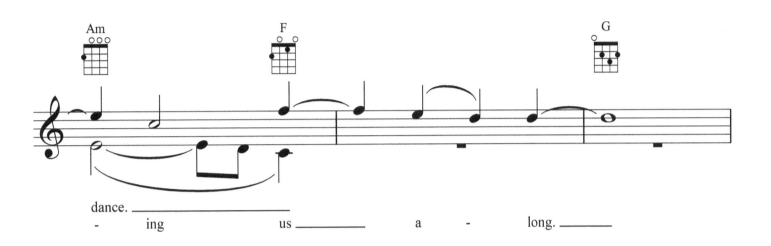

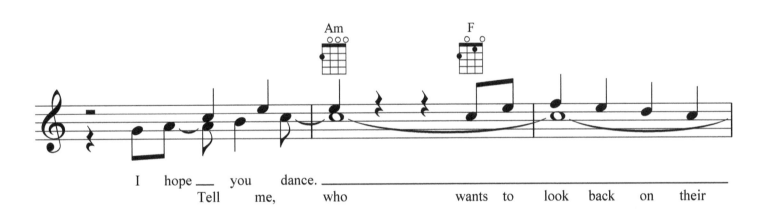

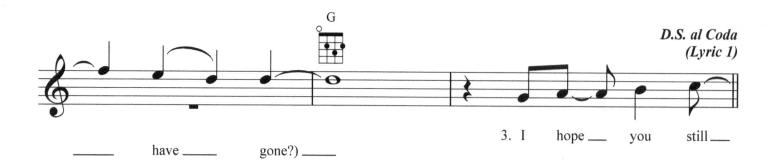

D.S. al Coda
(Lyric 1)

_____ have _____ gone?) _____

3. I hope _____ you still _____

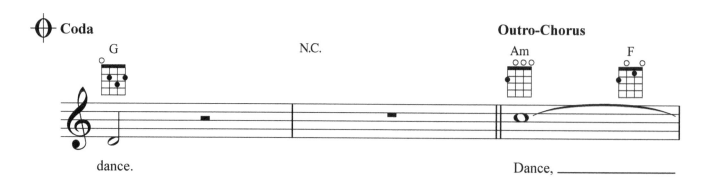

Coda

N.C.

Outro-Chorus

dance.

Dance, _____

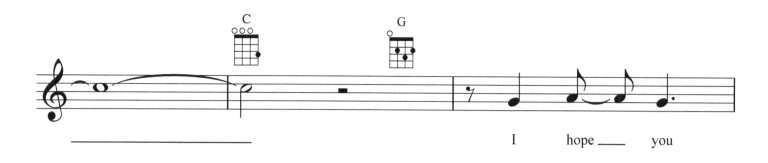

_____

I hope _____ you

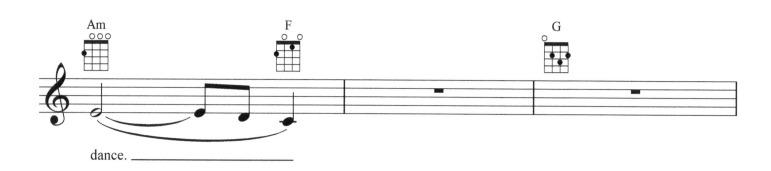

dance. _____

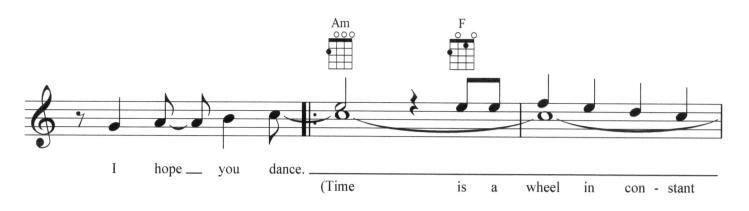

I hope _____ you dance. _____

(Time is a wheel in con - stant

I hope — you dance. _____
mo - tion, al - ways roll - ing us ___

I hope ___ you dance. ___
___ a - long. _____ Tell me,

who wants to look back on their youth and won -

I hope — you dance. _____
- der where ___ those years ___ have ___ gone?) ___

Repeat and fade

___ I hope ____ you dance. ___

I'm a Mess

Words and Music by Ed Sheeran

Ice Cream

Words and Music by Sarah McLachlan

If You Know What I Mean

Words and Music by Neil Diamond

First note

Verse
Moderately

1. When the night re - turns just like a friend,

when the eve - ning comes to set me free, _____

when the qui - et hours that wait be - yond the day make

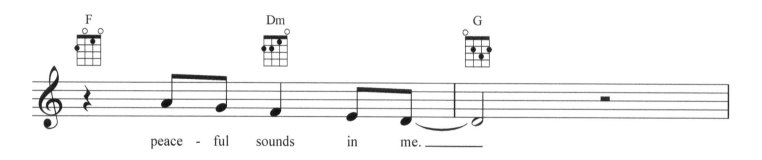

peace - ful sounds in me. _____

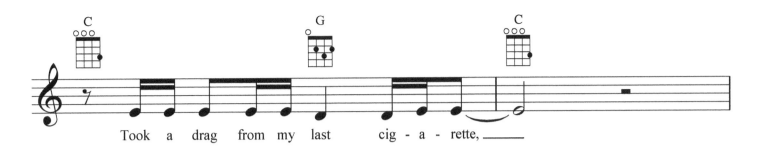

Took a drag from my last cig - a - rette, _____

took a drink from a glass of old _____ wine.

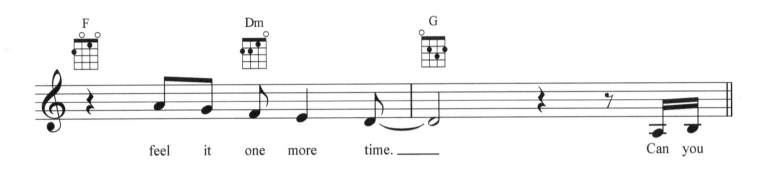

I closed my eyes, and I could make it real and

feel it one more time. _____ Can you

𝄋 Pre-Chorus

hear it, babe? _
hear it, babe? _

Can you hear it, babe? _
Do you hear it, babe? _

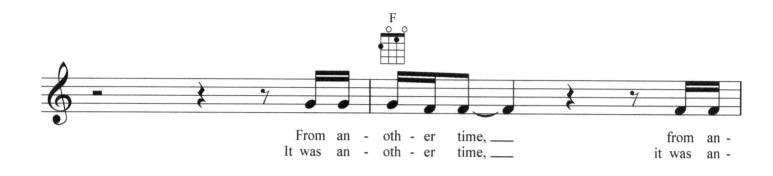

From an - oth - er time, ___ from an -
It was an - oth - er time, ___ it was an -

oth - er place, ___ do you re - mem - ber it, babe?
oth - er place. ___ Do you re - mem - ber it, babe?

Chorus

And the ra - di - o played like a car - ni - val

tune as we lay in our bed in the oth - er

room, when we gave it a - way for the sake of a

70

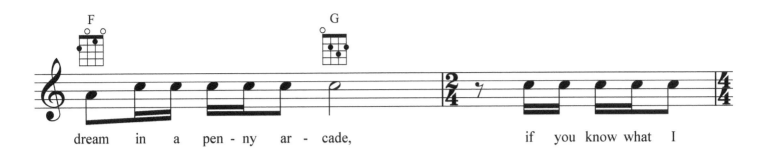

dream in a pen - ny ar - cade, if you know what I

Fine

mean. 2. Here's to the songs we used to

sing, and here's to the times we used ___ to know. ___

It's hard to hold them in our arms a - gain but

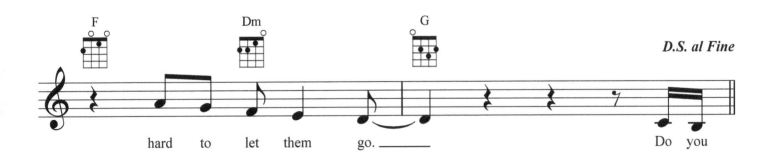

D.S. al Fine

hard to let them go. _____ Do you

Last Night I Had the Strangest Dream

Words and Music by Ed McCurdy

(Can't Live Without Your)
Love and Affection

Words and Music by Marc Tanner, Matt Nelson and Gunnar Nelson

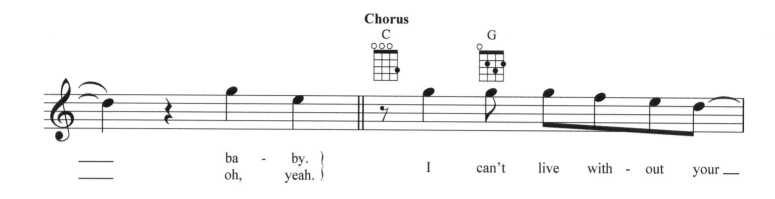

Chorus

ba - by.
oh, yeah.

I can't live with - out your —

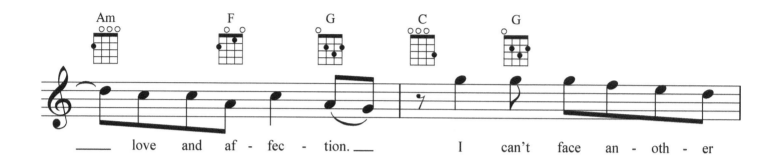

— love and af - fec - tion. — I can't face an - oth - er

night on my own. I'd give up my pride to save me from be - ing a -

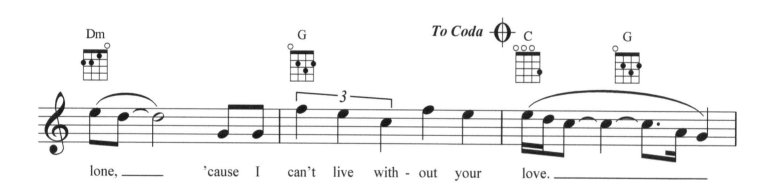

To Coda

lone, _____ 'cause I can't live with - out your love. _____

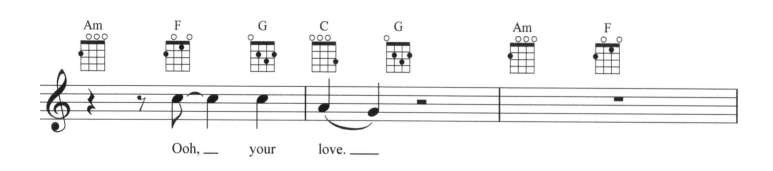

Ooh, __ your love. __

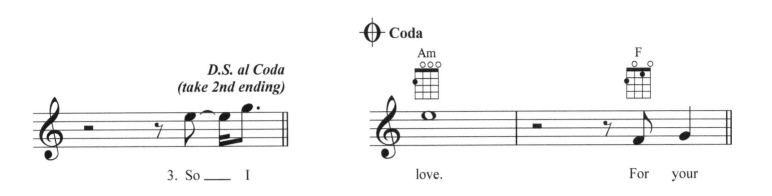

D.S. al Coda
(take 2nd ending)

Coda

3. So ___ I   love.   For your

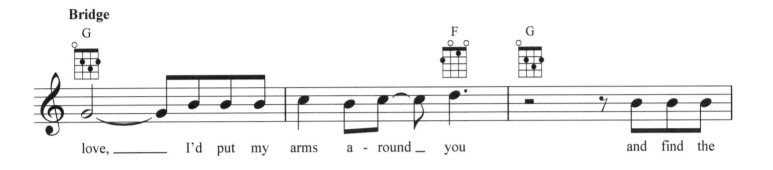

Bridge

love, _____ I'd put my arms a - round __ you   and find the

strength to tell __ you _____   that I can't live with - out your

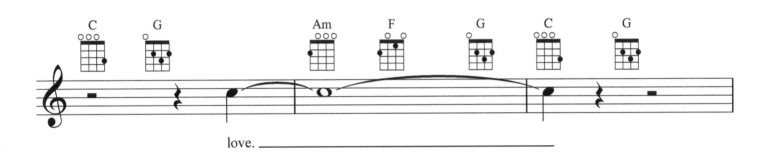

love. _____

Chorus

I can't live with - out your ___ love and af - fec - tion.

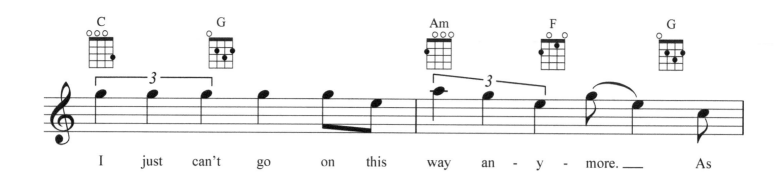

I just can't go on this way an-y-more. ___ As

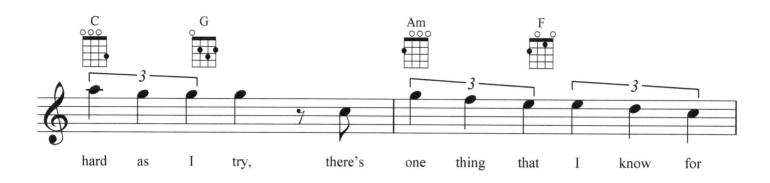

hard as I try, there's one thing that I know for

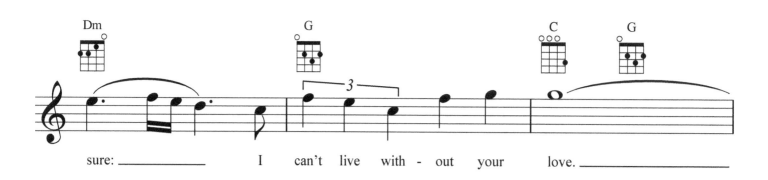

sure: _____ I can't live with - out your love. _____

Outro

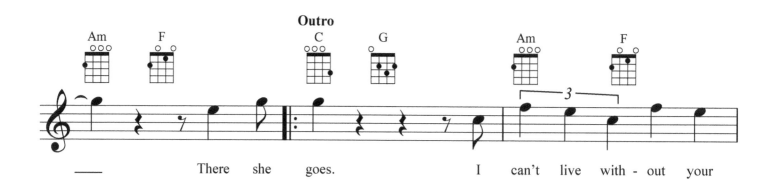

___ There she goes. I can't live with - out your

Repeat and fade

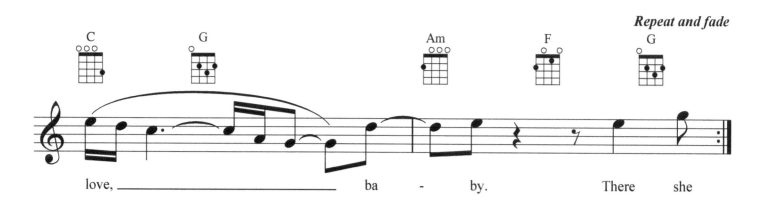

love, _____ ba - by. There she

Lollipop

Words and Music by Beverly Ross and Julius Dixon

Chorus

To Coda

C

Lol - li - pop. *(Instrumental)*

G

Bridge

F

Sweet - er than can - dy on a stick. ____

C   F   C

Huck - le - ber - ry, cher - ry or lime; _____

F

if you had a choice, she'd be your pick, ____ but

G   *D.C. al Coda*

Lol - li - pop is mine. _____ Oh,

Coda

G   C

(Instrumental)

Love Can Build a Bridge

Words and Music by Paul Overstreet, John Jarvis and Naomi Judd

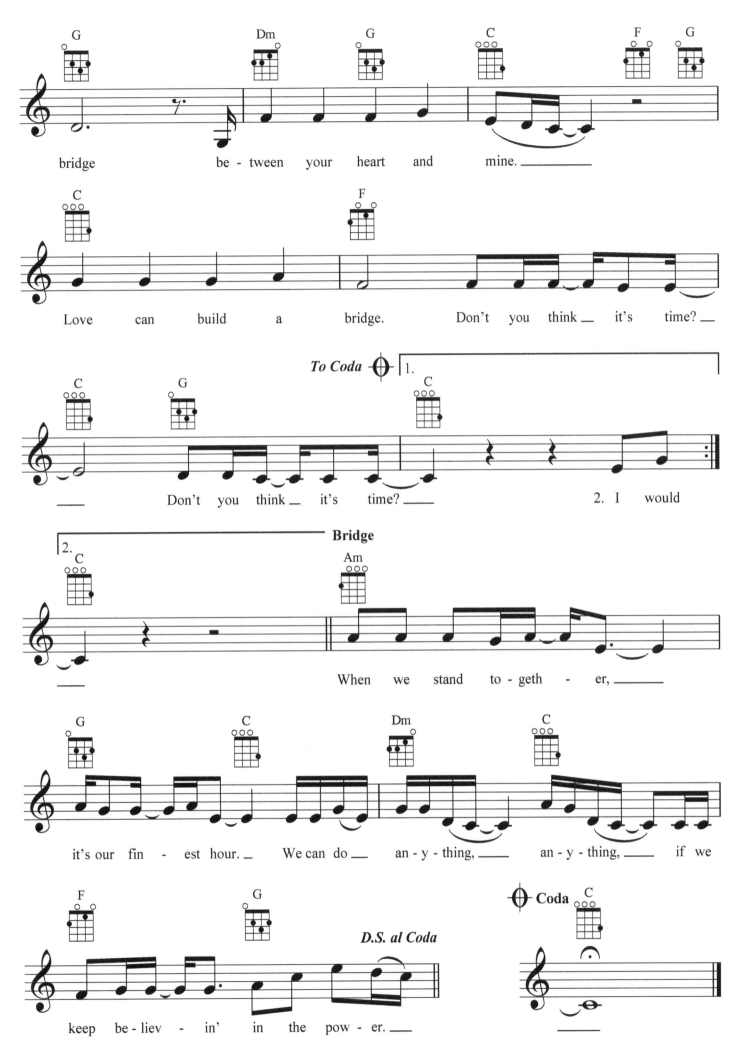

bridge be - tween your heart and mine. _____

Love can build a bridge. Don't you think __ it's time? __

To Coda ⊕ | 1.

__ Don't you think __ it's time? _____ 2. I would

Bridge

2. When we stand to - geth - er, _____

it's our fin - est hour. __ We can do __ an - y - thing, _____ an - y - thing, _____ if we

D.S. al Coda

⊕ **Coda**

keep be - liev - in' in the pow - er. __

Meet Virginia

Words and Music by Pat Monahan, James Stafford and Rob Hotchkiss

First note

Verse
Moderately, in 2

1. She does-n't own a dress. __ Her hair __ is al-
2. Smokes a pack a day. __ Wait, that's me; but an-

-ways a mess. If you catch her steal-in', she won't con-fess.
-y - way, __ she does-n't care a thing a-bout that. Hey,

She's beau-ti - ful. _____
she thinks I'm beau-ti - ful. _____ Meet Vir-gin - ia.

Verse

3. She nev - er com - pro - mis - es, loves ba - bies and __
5. Well, here __ she is _____ a - gain on the phone. Just like me, __

al - li - ga - tors.   Ma - ma works on car - bu - re - tors.

Her broth - er is a fine _____ me - di - a - tor   for the

D.S. al Coda

pres - i - dent.

Coda

"I don't real - ly wan - na live ____ this life.

Verse

6. She on - ly ____ drinks cof - fee ____ at mid - night   when the
7. You see, ____ her con - fi - dence is trag - ic,   but her

mo - ment is not _____ right   and her tim - ing is quite ____
in - tu - i - tion mag - ic   and the shape ___ of her bod -

Interlude

_____ un - u - su - al. _____
y   un - u - su - al. _____   Meet Vir - gin - ia.

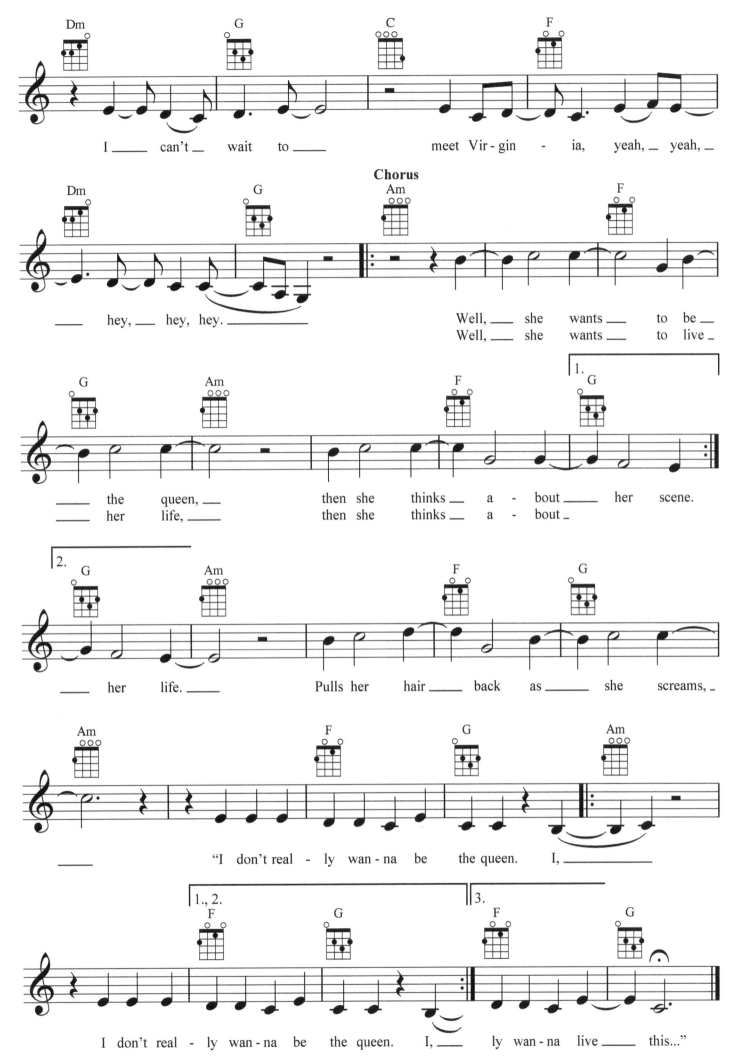

Mr. Jones

Words and Music by Adam Duritz, David Bryson, Charles Gillingham,
Matthew Malley, Steve Bowman, Daniel Vickrey and Ben Mize

_____ want some - thing beau - ti - ful.

Man, I wish I was beau -

ti - ful.

So, come dance this si - lence down _____ through the morn - ing.

Sha - la - la - la - la - la - la - la, _____ yeah.

Uh - huh, yeah. _____

Verse

2. Cut up, Ma - ri - a!

Show me some of them _ Span -

(3.) will paint my pic - ture,

paint my - self in blue and

- ish danc - es.

Pass _____ me a bot - tle, Mis - ter Jones.

red and black and gray.

All of the beau - ti - ful col - ors are ver - y, ver - y

Chorus

Smil - ing in the bright ___ lights, com - ing through in ster -
Stand - ing in the spot - light, I bought my - self a gray

e - o. When ev - 'ry - bod - y loves _____ you, ___
gui - tar. When ev - 'ry - bod - y loves _____ me, ___

1.
you can nev - er be lone - ly. ___ 3. Well, I

2.
I will nev - er be lone -

Bridge

- ly. _____ I will nev - er be lone -

- ly. Said, I'm _____ nev - er gon - na be

lone - ly.

I wan-na be a li-on. Yeah, ev-'ry-bod-

y wan-na pass ___ as cats. We all wan-na be big, ___ big stars, ___ yeah but,

we got dif-f'rent rea - sons for that. Be-lieve ___ in me

'cause I don't be-lieve ___ in an - y-thing, and I ___

___ wan-na be some - one to ___ be-lieve, to be-lieve, to ___

Chorus

___ be-lieve, yeah. ___ Mis - ter Jones and ___ me,
Mis - ter Jones and ___ me

Please Come to Boston

Words and Music by Dave Loggins

First note

Verse
Moderately slow

1. Please come to Bos - ton for the spring - time. I'm
2. Please come to Den - ver with the snow - fall. We'll
3. Please come to L. ___ A. to live for - ev - er. A

stay - ing here ___ with some friends ___ and they've ___ got lots ___ of room, ___ and
move up in - to the moun - tains ___ so far ___ that we can't be found, ___ and
Cal - i - for - nia life a - lone is just ___ too hard ___ to build. ___ I

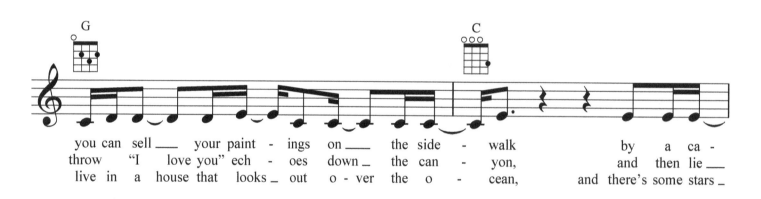

you can sell ___ your paint - ings on ___ the side - walk by a ca -
throw "I love you" ech - oes down ___ the can - yon, and then lie ___
live in a house that looks ___ out o - ver the o - cean, and there's some stars ___

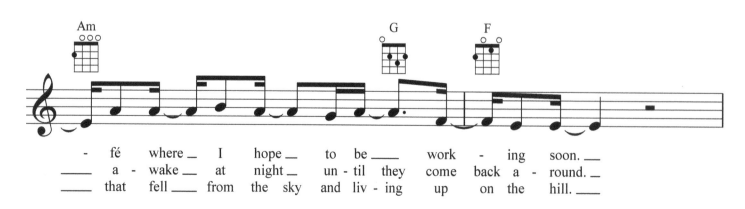

- fé where ___ I hope ___ to be ___ work - ing soon. ___
___ a - wake ___ at night ___ un - til they come back a - round. ___
___ that fell ___ from the sky and liv - ing up on the hill. ___

Please come to Bos - ton. She said, "No, _____ would you come home _ to me?" _
Please come to Den - ver. She said, "No, _____ would you come home _ to me?" _
Please come to L. _____ A. She said, "No, _____ would you come home _ to me?" _

Chorus

_____ And she said, _ "Hey, ram - blin' boy, _ now won't you set - tle down?
_____ And she said, _ "Hey, ram - blin' boy, _ why don't you set - tle down?
_____ And she said, _ "Hey, ram - blin' boy, _ why don't you set - tle down?

Bos - ton ain't _ your kind of town. _ } There ain't no gold _ and there ain't _ no - bod - y like
Den - ver ain't _ your kind of town. _ }
L.   A. can't be your kind of town. _ }

To Coda

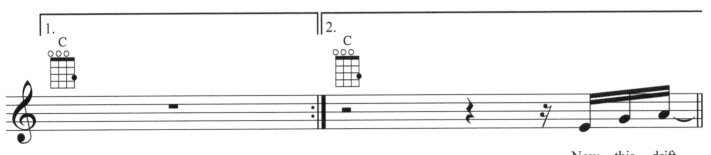

me. _____ I'm the num - ber one fan _ of the man _ from Ten - nes - see."

1.

2.

Now this drift -

Bridge

-er's world _ goes round _ and round _ and I doubt _ that it's ev-er gon-na stop. _ But of all _

_____ the dreams _ I've lost _ or found _ and all _____ that I ___ ain't got, _ I still need to

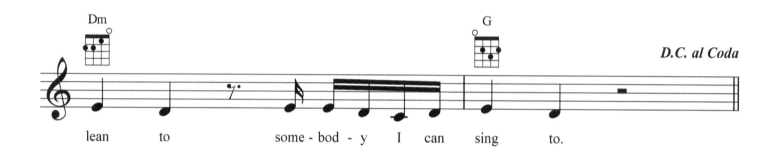

D.C. al Coda

lean to some-bod - y I can sing to.

Coda

Outro

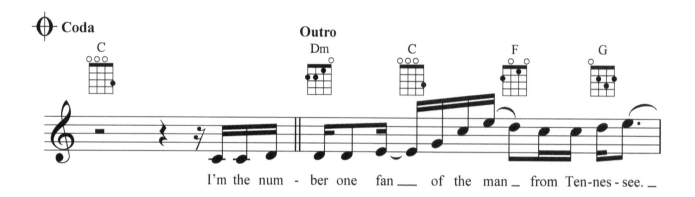

I'm the num - ber one fan _ of the man _ from Ten-nes-see.

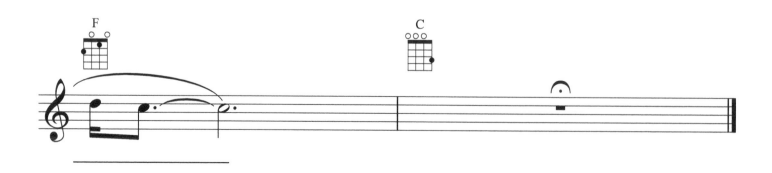

One Dream

Words and Music by Sarah McLachlan and Pierre Marchand

First note

Verse
Moderately, with feeling

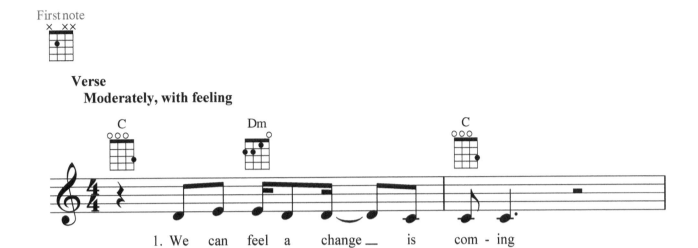

1. We can feel a change __ is com - ing

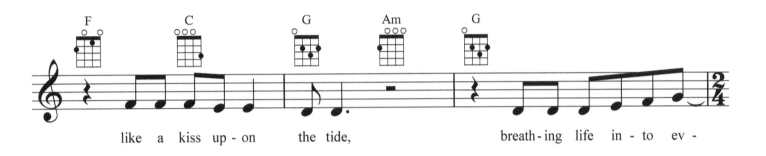

like a kiss up - on the tide, breath - ing life in - to ev -

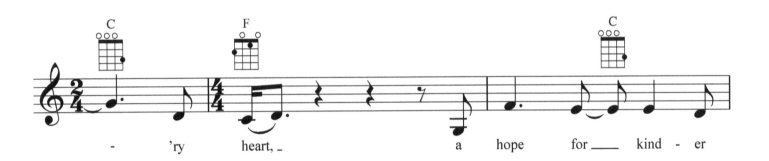

- 'ry heart, __ a hope for __ kind - er

times. 'Cause we all walk __ this road to - geth -

- er, though at times ___ we felt a -

lone. In the strug - gle to lift _____ us

up, ___ we find a strength un - yet de - fined. You

𝄋 Pre-Chorus

car - ry your cour - age, car - ry the his - t'ry

of all who've gone ___ be - fore ___ you. Wher -

ev - er you come ___ from, you're born ___ of the one ___ dream that finds ___

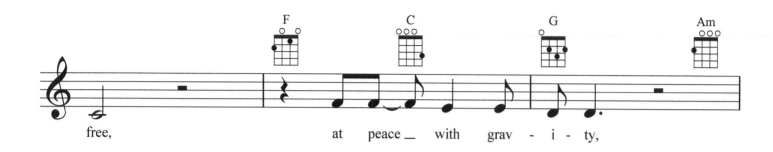

free,   at peace __ with   grav - i - ty,

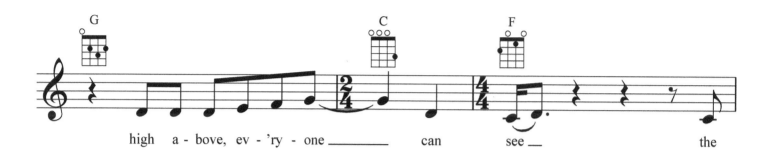

high a - bove, ev - 'ry - one _____ can   see __   the

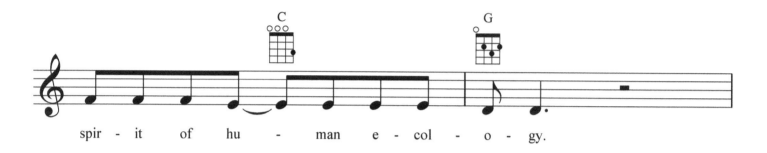

spir - it of hu - man e - col - o - gy.

How your flame _ keeps burn - ing   when you leave all   doubt _

_____ be - hind.   It's a gi - ant leap _____ for man -

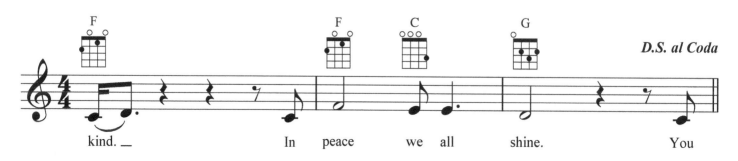

D.S. al Coda

kind. _   In peace we all   shine.   You

Poor Little Fool

Words and Music by Sharon Sheeley

First note

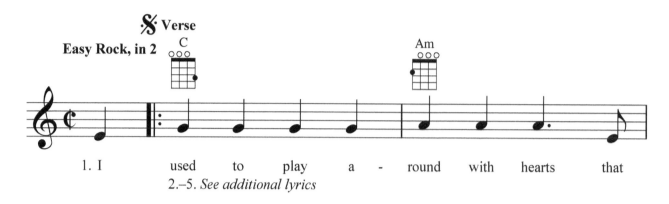

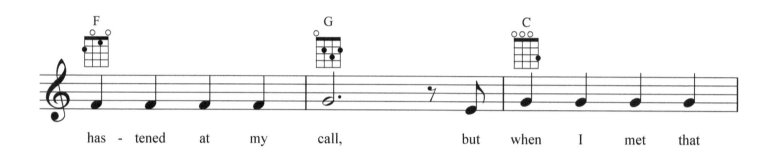

1. I used to play a - round with hearts that
2.–5. See additional lyrics

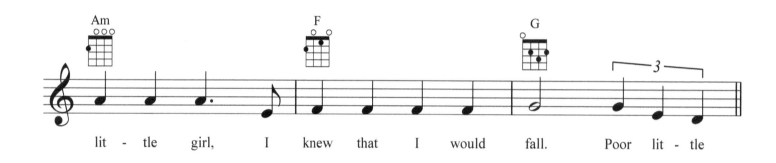

has - tened at my call, but when I met that

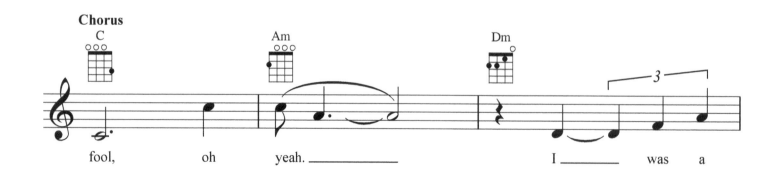

lit - tle girl, I knew that I would fall. Poor lit - tle

Chorus

fool, oh yeah. _____ I _____ was a

fool, _____ uh - huh. (Uh - huh, poor lit - tle fool.

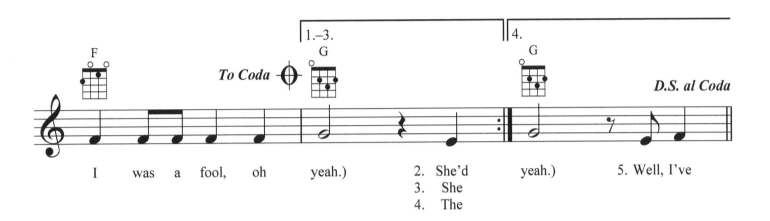

I was a fool, oh yeah.)   2. She'd   yeah.)   5. Well, I've
3. She
4. The

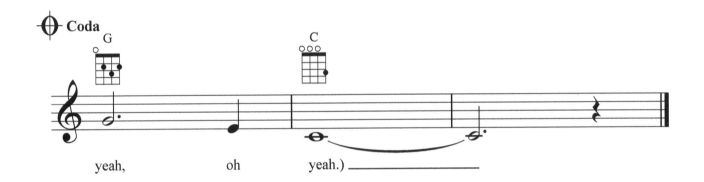

yeah,   oh   yeah.) _____

Additional Lyrics

2. She'd play around and tease me
   With her carefree devil eyes.
   She'd hold me close and kiss me,
   But her heart was full of lies.

3. She told me how she cared for me,
   That we'd never part.
   And so, for the very first time,
   I gave away my heart.

4. The next day she was gone,
   And I knew she lied to me.
   She left me with a broken heart,
   Won her victory.

5. Well, I've played this game with other hearts,
   But I never thought I'd see
   The day when someone else would play
   Love's foolish game with me.

The Real Love

Words and Music by Bob Seger

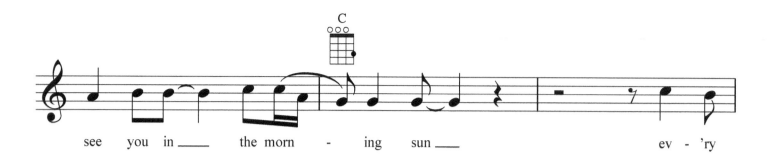

see you in ____ the morn - ing sun ____ ev - 'ry

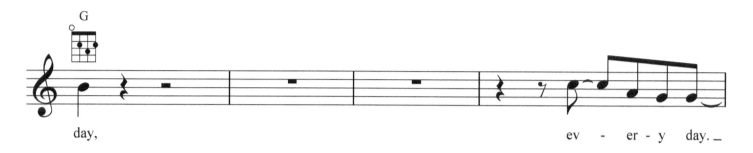

day, ev - er - y day. ___

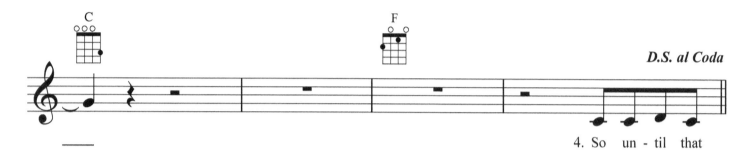

___ 4. So un - til that

D.S. al Coda

⊕ **Coda**

Real ___ love.

Un - til we've got the

Outro

Repeat and fade

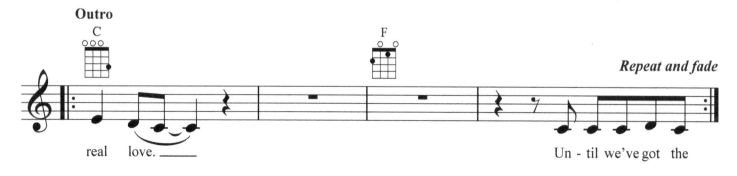

real love. ___ Un - til we've got the

Paradise

Words and Music by Guy Berryman, Jon Buckland, Will Champion, Chris Martin and Brian Eno

par - a - par - a - par - a - dise, par - a - par - a - - par - a - dise, par - a - par - a - par - a - dise.

Bridge

Oh, _____ oh. _____ La, la, _____ la, la, la,

la, la, _____ la, la, la, la, la, _____ la, la, la, _____ la, la. _____ And so ly -

- ing un - der - neath _____ those storm - y skies, _____

_____ she said, "Oh, _____ I know the

Right Here Waiting

Words and Music by Richard Marx

First note

Verse
Moderate Ballad

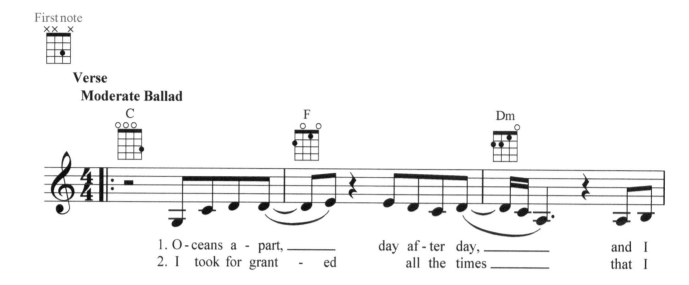

1. O - ceans a - part, _____ day af - ter day, _____ and I
2. I took for grant - ed all the times _____ that I

slow - ly go ____ in - sane. ___ I hear your voice _____ on the line, _
thought would last ___ some - how. ___ I hear the laugh - ter, I taste the tears, _

Pre-Chorus

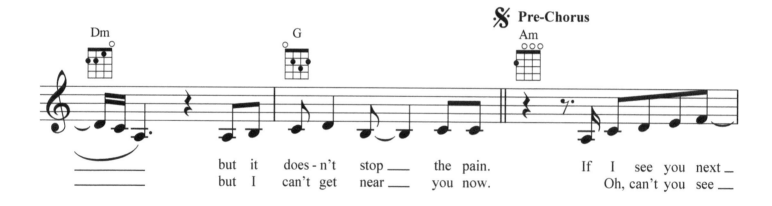

_____ but it does - n't stop ___ the pain. If I see you next _
_____ but I can't get near ___ you now. Oh, can't you see _

____ to nev - er, _____ how can we say ____ for - ev - er? ___
____ it, ba - by? _____ You've got me go - in' cra - zy. ___

end, if I'm ___ with you, ___ I'll take ___ the chance. ___

Interlude

D.S. al Coda
(Lyric 2)

Coda
Outro

Wait - ing for you. ___

Redemption Song

Words and Music by Bob Marley

Additional Lyrics

2., 3. Emancipate yourselves from mental slavery;
None but ourselves can free our minds.
Have no fear for atomic energy,
'Cause none of them can stop the time.
How long shall they kill our prophets
While we stand aside and look?
Some say it's just a part of it;
We've got to fulfill the Book.

Slow Dancing in a Burning Room

Words and Music by John Mayer

hit me just to hurt me so you leave me feel-ing dirt-y 'cause you

Chorus

can't un-der-stand. We're go - ing ___ down, _____ and you can

see it, too. ___ We're go - ing ___ down, _____ and you

know that we're doomed. _ My dear, ___ we're _ slow danc-ing in a

Interlude

burn - ing room. _ *(Instrumental)*

1.

2. I was the

2.

Go

She's So High

Words and Music by Tal Bachman

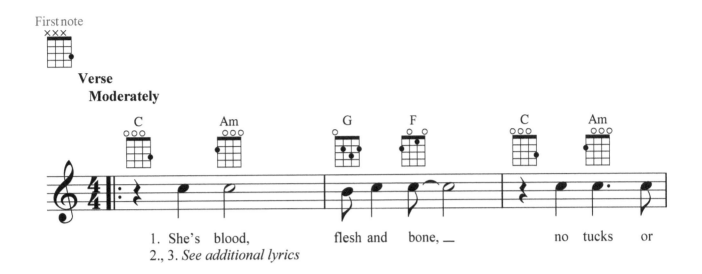

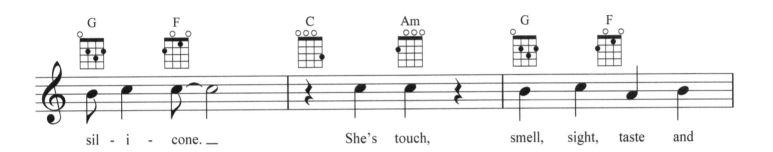

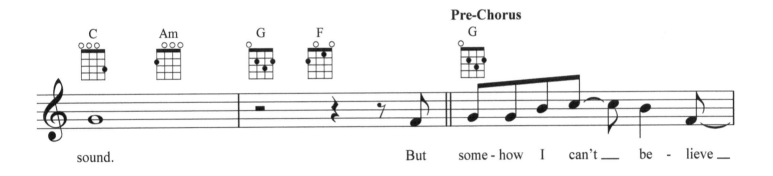

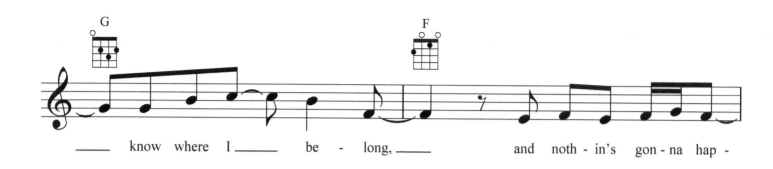

___ know where I ___ be - long, ___ and noth - in's gon - na hap -

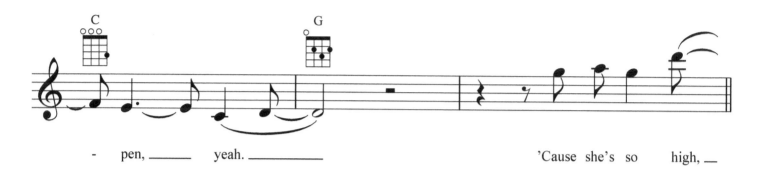

- pen, ___ yeah. ___ 'Cause she's so high, ___

Chorus

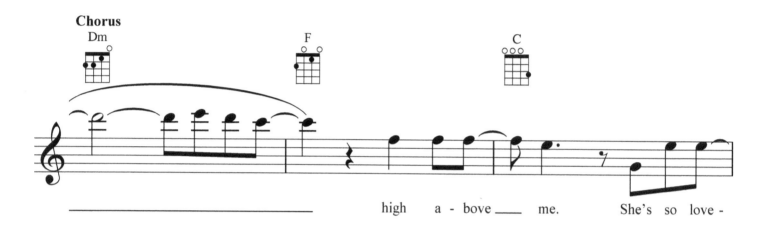

___ high a - bove ___ me. She's so love -

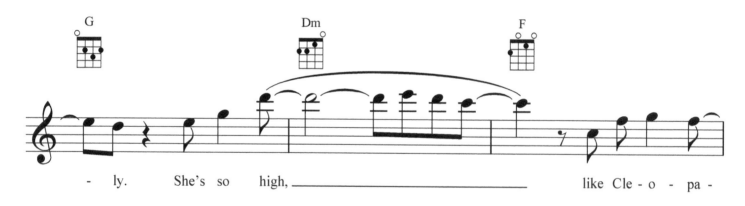

- ly. She's so high, ___ like Cle - o - pa -

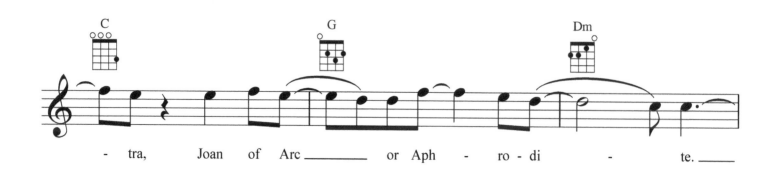

- tra, Joan of Arc ___ or Aph - ro - di - te. ___

Do, do, do, ___ do, do. ___ She's so high, ___

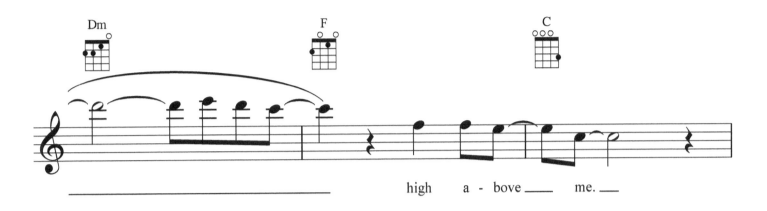

high a - bove ___ me. ___

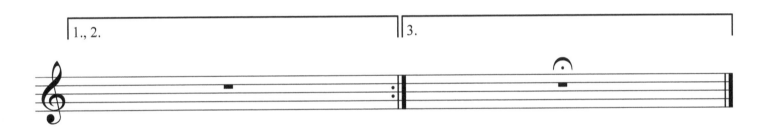

1., 2.

3.

Additional Lyrics

2. First-class and fancy-free, she's high society.
   She's got the best of everything.
   What could a guy like me ever really offer?
   She's perfect as she can be; why should I ever bother?

3. She calls to speak to me.
   I freeze immediately 'cause what she says sounds so unreal.
   'Cause somehow I can't believe that anything should happen.
   I know where I belong, and nothing's gonna happen.

Slow Hand

Words and Music by Michael Clark and John Bettis

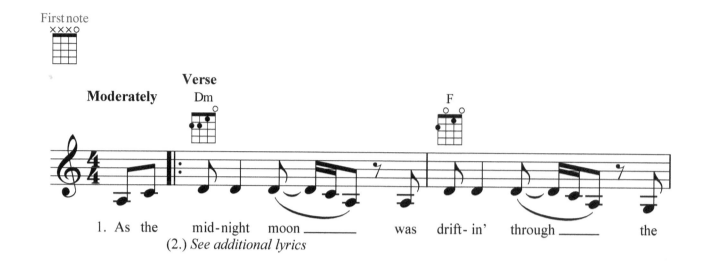

1. As the mid-night moon _____ was drift-in' through _____ the
(2.) *See additional lyrics*

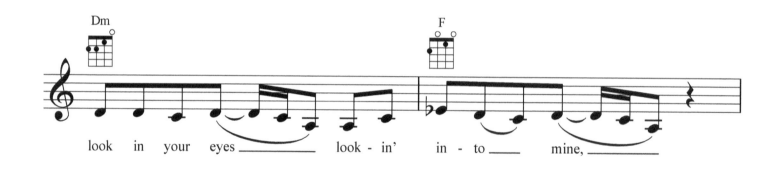

la - zy sway _____ of the trees, _____ I saw the

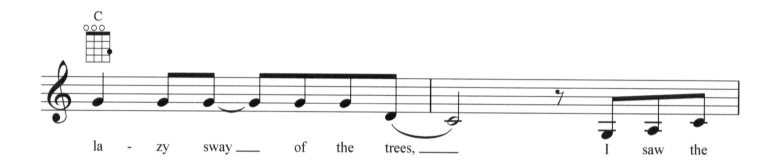

look in your eyes _____ look - in' in - to _____ mine,

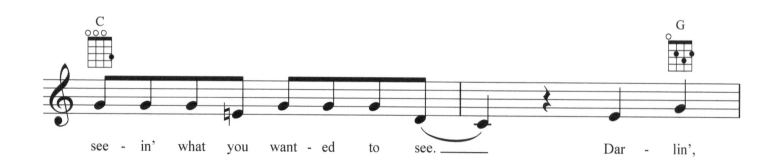

see - in' what you want - ed to see. _____ Dar - lin',

don't say a word, ____ 'cause I al - read - y heard ____ what your

bod - y's say - in' to mine. ____ I'm tired of

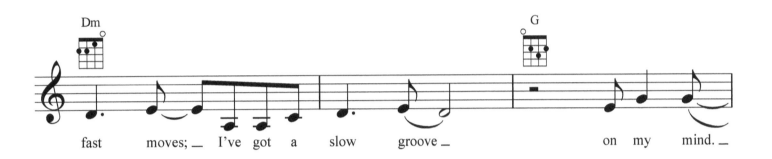

fast moves; __ I've got a slow groove __ on my mind. __

%· **Chorus**

I want a man __ with a slow hand. __
(2., 3.) See additional lyrics

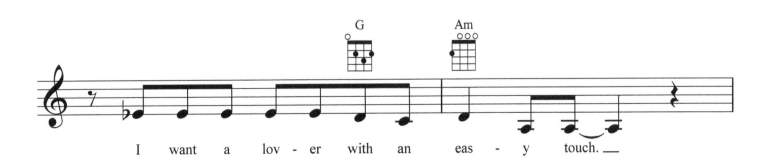

I want a lov - er with an eas - y touch. __

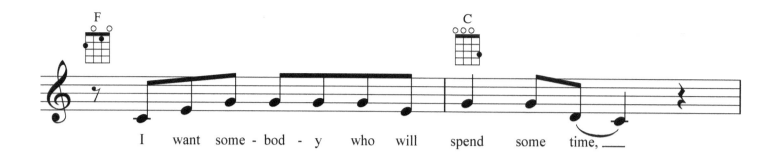

I want some-bod-y who will spend some time, ___

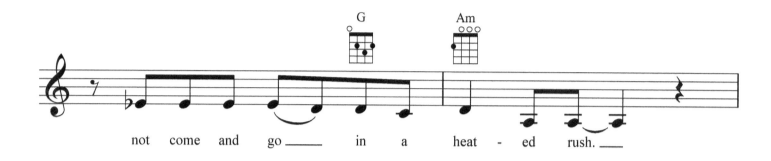

not come and go ___ in a heat-ed rush. ___

I want some-bod-y who will un-der-stand ___

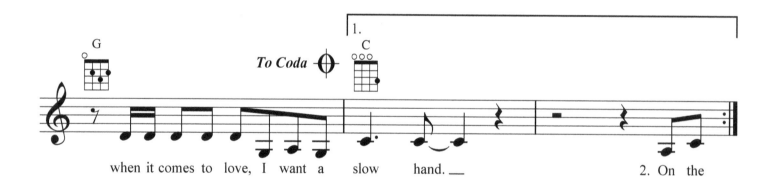

To Coda

1.

when it comes to love, I want a slow hand. ___   2. On the

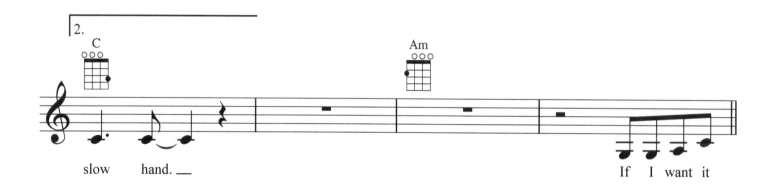

2.

slow hand. ___   If I want it

Bridge

all night, ___ please ___ say it's all right. ___

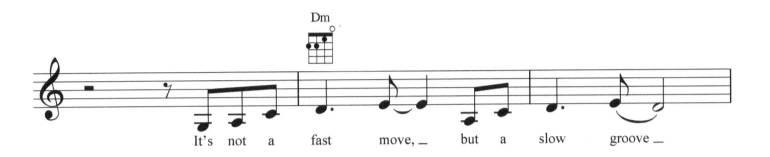

It's not a fast move, ___ but a slow groove ___

D.S. al Coda

on my mind. _____ 'Cause I got a man ___ with a

Coda

slow hand. _____

Additional Lyrics

2. On the shadowed ground, with no one around, and a blanket of stars in our eyes,
   We are drifting free like two lost leaves on the crazy wind of the night.
   Darlin', don't say a word, 'cause I already heard what your body's sayin' to mine.
   If I want it all night, you say it's all right; we got the time.

Chorus: 'Cause I got a man with a slow hand, I got a lover with an easy touch.
   I got somebody who will spend some time, not come and go in a heated rush.
   I found somebody who will understand when it comes to love, I want a slow hand.

Some Nights

Words and Music by Jeff Bhasker, Andrew Dost, Jack Antonoff and Nate Ruess

who I am, ___ who I ___ am, who I am. _____ Oh,

who am I? _____ Mm, ___ mm. _____

Chorus

___ Well, some nights ___ I wish ___ that this

all ___ would end _____ 'cause I could use some friends ___ for a ___

___ change. And some nights ___ I'm scared ___ you'll for -

get me ___ a - gain. ___ Some nights I al - ways win, ___ I

al - ways win. But I still wake __ up, _____ I still

see your __ ghost. __ Oh, Lord, I'm still not __ sure _____ what I

stand for, __ oh. __ Whoa, _____ what do I stand for? __ What do I stand for? __

Most nights, __ I _____ don't know. _____ Oh, come on. __

Bridge 1

(Spoken:) So this is it.   I sold my soul for this?   Ooh, na, ___ na.
                                                                    Washed my hands of that for this?

Ooh, na, ___ na, come on. _____ Ooh, na, ___ na, come on. __
I miss my mom and dad for this?   No, when I see stars, when I see, when I see stars, that's all they are.

Ooh, na, __ na, they sound like __ this one, so come on. _____ Oh, come on. _

When I hear songs...

_____ Oh, come on. _____ Oh, __ come on. __ 3. Well,

Verse

that is it, __ guys, that is all. __ Five min - utes in and I'm bored a - gain.

Ten years of this, I'm not sure if an - y - bod - y un - der - stands. __ This

one is not __ for the folks at home. __ Sor - ry to leave, Mom, I had to go. __

Who the f**k wants to die a - lone, all dried up in __ the des - ert sun? __ My heart is

ah, _____

ah, _____   ah. _____

Outro-Verse

Coda

The oth - er night,   you would - n't   be - lieve   the   dream _

_____ I   just had   a - bout _ you   and   me.   I called you up,   but we both   a - gree.

It's for the best you did - n't   lis   -   ten. _____

It's for the best   we   get _ our   dis   -   tance, _   oh. _____

135

Stay

Words and Music by Mikky Ekko and Justin Parker

First note

1. All a - long __ it was a fe - ver.

A cold __ sweat, hot - head - ed be - liev - er.

2. I threw my hands in the air, __ said,
3. It's not much of a

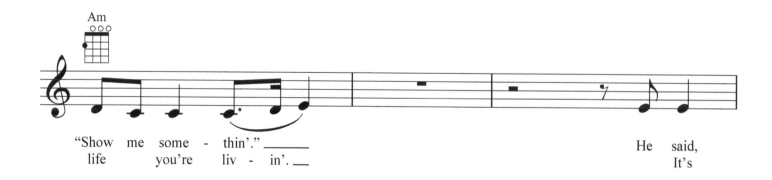

"Show me some - thin'." _____
life you're liv - in'. __

He said,
It's

"If you dare, ___ come a lit - tle clos - er."
not just some - thin' you take; it's giv - en.

Pre-Chorus

'Round and a - round and a - round and a - round we go. ___

Am   F

___   Oh, ___ now, tell me now, tell me

Dm   G

now, tell me now you know. ___

𝄋 Chorus

Not real - ly sure how to feel a - bout ___ it. Some - thin' in the way you move ___

___ makes ___ me feel like I can't ___ live with - out you. Well, it ___

'Cause when you nev - er see the light, it's

hard to know which one of us is cav - in'.

D.S. al Coda

Coda
Outro

Stay. _____

I want you to stay. _____

Ooh. _____

Sunday Mornin' Comin' Down

Words and Music by Kris Kristofferson

First note

Verse
Moderately, in 2

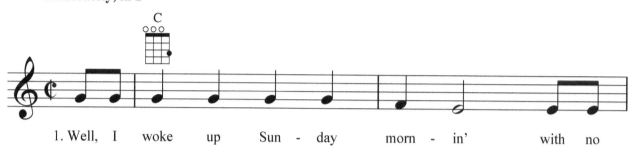

1. Well, I woke up Sun - day morn - in' with no

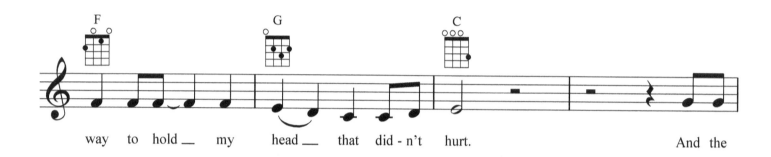

way to hold __ my head __ that did - n't hurt. And the

beer I had __ for break - fast was - n't bad, so I had one more for des -

sert. Then I fum - bled in my clos - et, through my

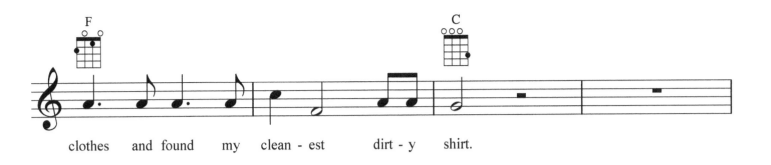

clothes and found my clean - est dirt - y shirt.

Then I washed my face ___ and combed my hair, ___

and stum-bled down the stairs ___ to meet the day. 2. I'd

Verse

smoked my mind ___ the night be - fore ___ with cig - a - rettes and
(3.) *See additional lyrics*

songs ___ I'd been pick - in'.

But I   lit   my   first ___   and   watched   a   small ___   kid

Am   G

play-in' ___   with   a   can ___   that   he   was   kick-in'.

C

Then   I   walked   a - cross ___   the

F

street ___   and   caught   the   Sun - day   smell ___   of   some - one's ___

C   Am

fry - in'   chick - en.   And,   Lord,   it

F   G   Dm

took   me   back ___   to   some - thin'   that   I   lost   some - where, ___

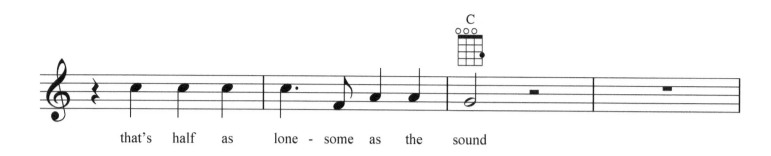

that's half as lone - some as the sound

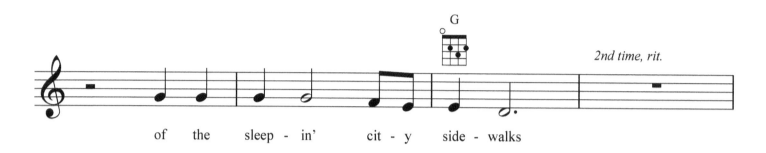

of the sleep - in' cit - y side - walks

2nd time, rit.

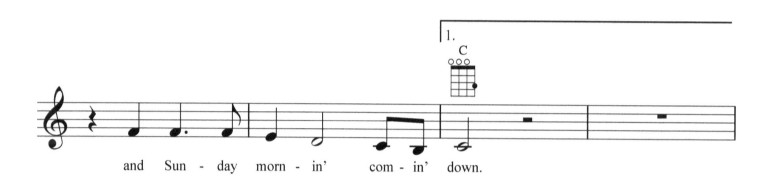

1.

and Sun - day morn - in' com - in' down.

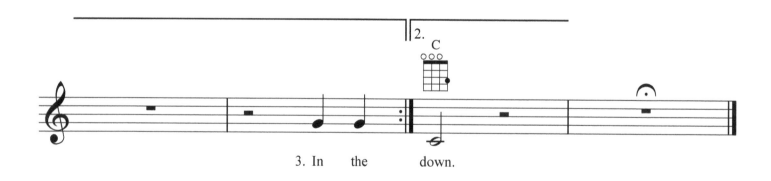

2.

3. In the down.

Additional Lyrics

3. In the park I saw a daddy with a laughin' little girl that he was swingin',
And I stopped beside a Sunday school and listened to the songs they were singin'.
Then I headed down the streets, and somewhere far away a lonely bell was ringin',
And it echoed through the canyons like the disappearing dreams of yesterday.

Waiting on the World to Change

Words and Music by John Mayer

First note

1. Me and all my friends, _ we're all _ mis - un - der - stood. _ They
(2.) *See additional lyrics*

say we stand for noth - ing and _ there's no way we ev - er could. Now, we see

ev - 'ry - thing that's go - ing wrong _ with the

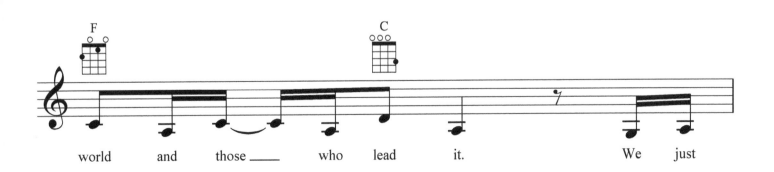

world and those _ who lead it. We just

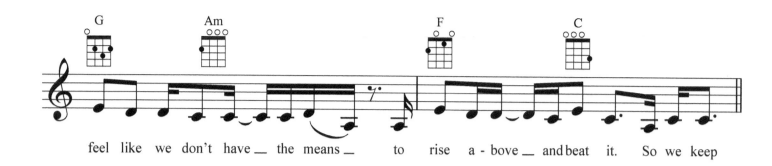

feel like we don't have __ the means __ to rise a - bove __ and beat it. So we keep

𝄋 Chorus

wait - ing (wait - ing), ____ wait - ing on the world __ to change. We keep on

wait - ing (wait - ing), ____ wait - ing on the world __ to change.

{ It's
{ It's
{ One

hard to beat __ the sys - tem when we're stand - ing at ____ a dis - tance. So we keep
not that we __ don't care; __ we just know that the fight ain't fair. So we keep on
day our gen - er - a - tion is gon - na rule the pop - u - la - tion. So we keep on

To Coda ⊕ |1.

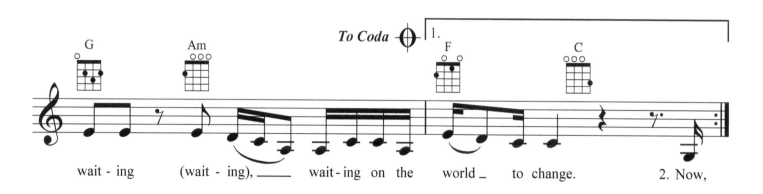

wait - ing (wait - ing), ____ wait - ing on the world __ to change. 2. Now,

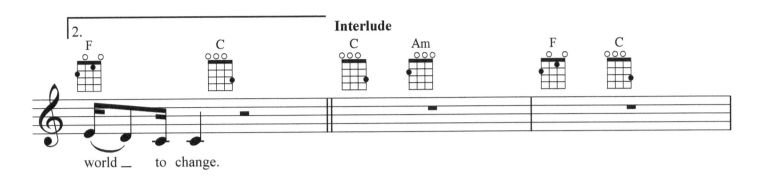

world __ to change.

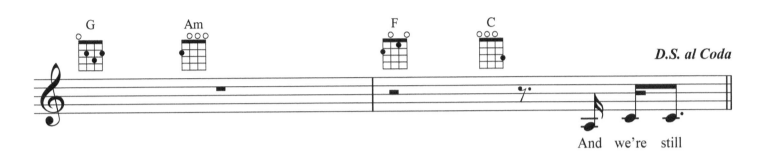

And we're still

world __ to change, wait-ing on the world __ to change, wait-ing on the

world __ to change, wait-ing on the world __ to change.

Additional Lyrics

2. Now, if we had the power to bring our neighbors home from war,
They would have never missed a Christmas; no more ribbons on their door.
And when you trust your television, what you get is what you got.
'Cause when they own the information, oh, they can bend it all they want.
That's why we're... *(Chorus)*

Superheroes

Words and Music by Danny O'Donoghue, Mark Sheehan and James Barry

First note

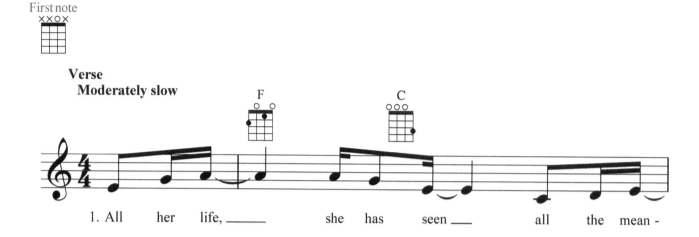

Verse
Moderately slow

1. All her life, _____ she has seen _____ all the mean-

-er side _____ of mean. _____ They took a-way _____ the proph-et's dream _____ for a prof-

-it on _____ the street. _____ Now she's strong-er than you know; _____ a heart of

steel _____ starts to grow. _____ 2. All his life, _____ he's been told _____ he'll be noth-
(3.) _____ all the lies, _____ all the tears _____

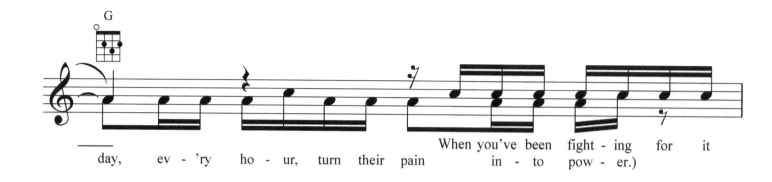

day, ev - 'ry ho - ur, turn their pain in - to pow - er.)

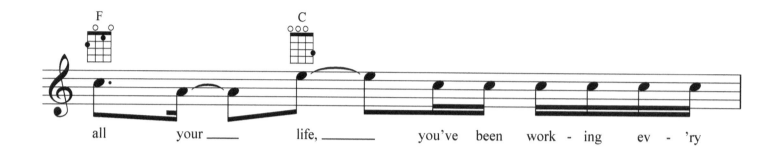

When you've been fight - ing for it all your ____ life, _____ you've been work - ing ev - 'ry

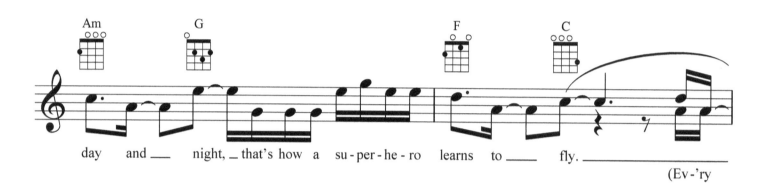

day and ___ night, ___ that's how a su - per - he - ro learns to ___ fly. _____ (Ev -'ry

1.

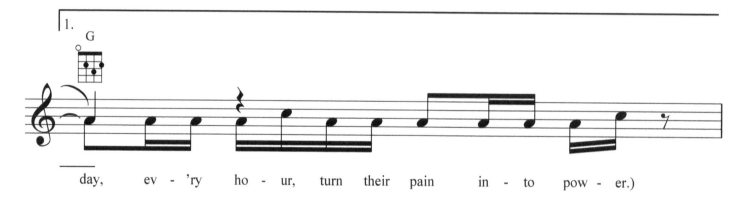

day, ev - 'ry ho - ur, turn their pain in - to pow - er.)

(Oh, uh oh. ___ Oh, oh, _____ uh oh.) ___ 3. All the hurt, ___

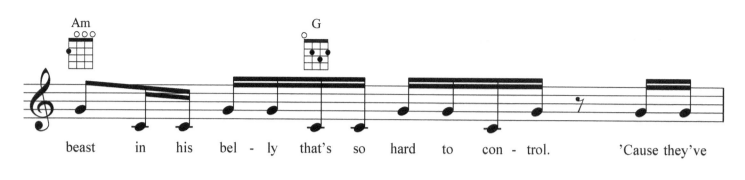

beast in his bel - ly that's so hard to con - trol. 'Cause they've

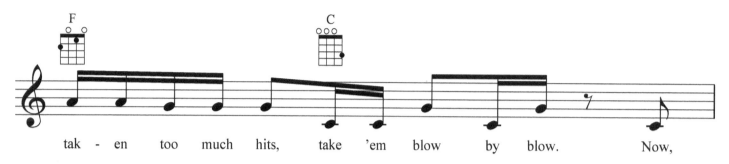

tak - en too much hits, take 'em blow by blow. Now,

light a match, stand back, watch 'em ex - plode. She's got

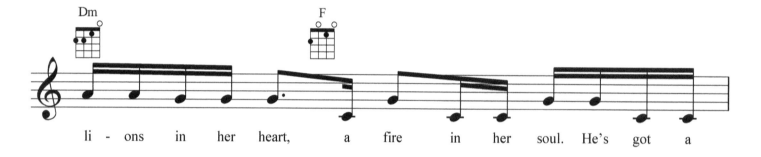

li - ons in her heart, a fire in her soul. He's got a

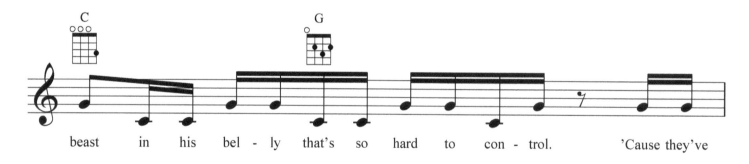

beast in his bel - ly that's so hard to con - trol. 'Cause they've

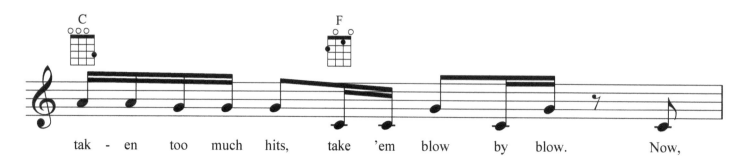

tak - en too much hits, take 'em blow by blow. Now,

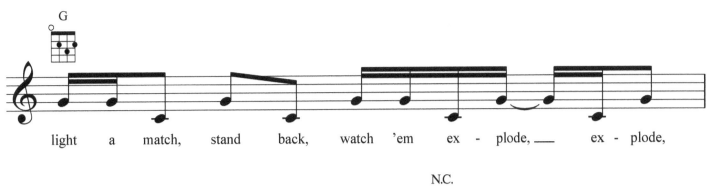

light   a   match,   stand   back,   watch 'em ex - plode, ___   ex - plode,

N.C.

D.S. al Coda
(take 2nd ending)

ex - plode,   ex - plode,   ex - plode.   When you've been fight - ing   for   it

Coda

day,   ev - 'ry ho - ur, turn their pain   in - to pow - er.)
When you've been fight - ing   for   it

all   your ___   life, ___   you've been strug - gl - ing   to

make   things ___   right, ___   that's how   a   su - per - he - ro

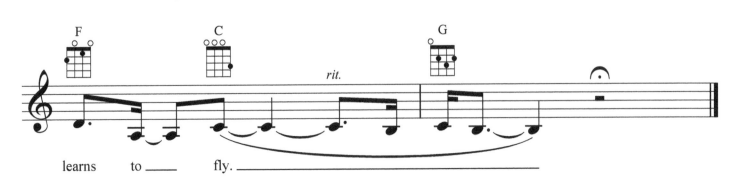

rit.

learns   to ___   fly. ___

The Times They Are A-Changin'

Words and Music by Bob Dylan

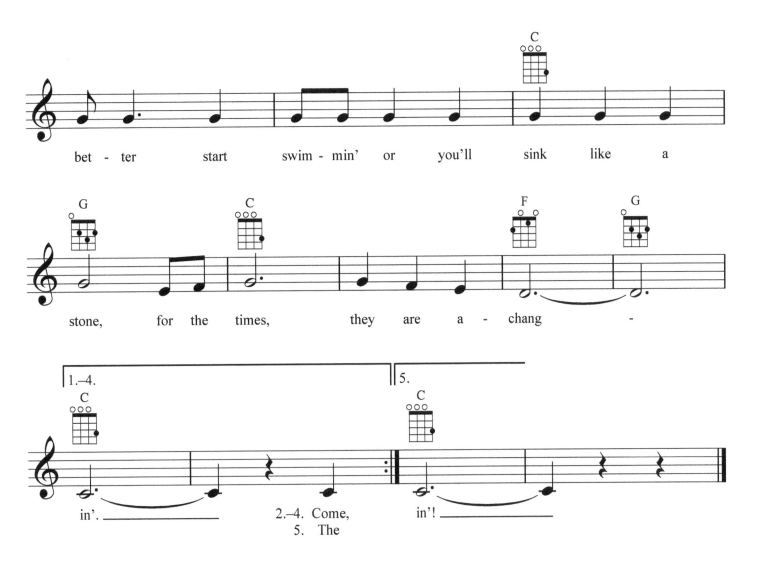

bet - ter start swim - min' or you'll sink like a

stone, for the times, they are a - chang -

1.–4.
in'. _____ 2.–4. Come,
5. The

5.
in'! _____

Additional Lyrics

2. Come, writers and critics who prophesy with your pen,
   And keep your eyes wide; the chance won't come again.
   And don't speak too soon, for the wheel's still in spin,
   And there's no tellin' who that it's namin'.
   For the loser now will be later to win,
   For the times, they are a-changin'.

3. Come, senators, congressmen, please heed the call.
   Don't stand in the doorway, don't block up the hall.
   For he that gets hurt will be he who has stalled.
   There's a battle outside and it's ragin'.
   It'll soon shake your windows and rattle your walls,
   For the times, they are a-changin'!

4. Come, mothers and fathers throughout the land,
   And don't criticize what you can't understand.
   Your sons and your daughters are beyond your command;
   Your old road is rapidly agin'.
   Please get out of the new one if you can't lend your hand,
   For the times, they are a-changin'!

5. The line it is drawn, the curse it is cast.
   The slow one now will later be fast.
   As the present now will later be past,
   The order is rapidly fadin'.
   And the first one now will later be last,
   For the times, they are a-changin'!

Turning Tables

Words and Music by Adele Adkins and Ryan Tedder

heart you think __ you gave __ me. _____ It's time to say good - bye __

Let chord ring.

__ to turn - ing ta - bles, _____

To Coda

1. *to turn - ing ta - bles. _____*

2. *_____ turn - ing ta - bles. _____*

Bridge

Next time, __ I'll __

__ be brav - er. I'll be __ my __ own sav - ior when the

thun - der calls __ for me. _____ Next time, __ I'll __ be brav - er. I'll be __ my __ own sav - ior, stand - ing __ on my own __ two feet. _____

*G

N.C.

D.S. al Coda

* Let chord ring.

Coda

to turn - ing ta - bles. _____

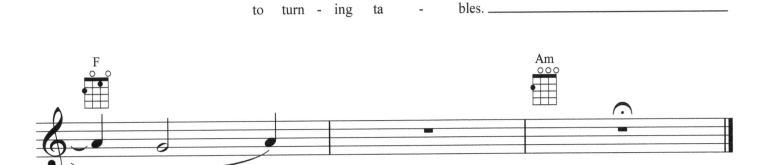

Additional Lyrics

2. Under hardest guise I see, ooh,
   Where love is lost, your ghost is found.
   I braved a hundred storms to leave you.
   As hard as you try, no, I will never be knocked down.

We Didn't Start the Fire

Words and Music by Billy Joel

First note

Verse
Bright Rock

C   G

1. Har - ry Tru - man, Dor - is Day,   Red Chi - na, John - nie Ray,

Am   F

South Pa - cif - ic, Wal - ter Win - chell, Joe Di - Mag - gi - o.

C   G

Joe Mc - Car - thy, Rich - ard Nix - on, Stu - de - bak - er, tel - e - vi - sion,

Am   F

North Ko - re - a, South Ko - re - a, Mar - i - lyn Mon - roe.

Verse

C   G

2. Ro - sen - bergs,   H - Bomb,   Sug - ar Ray,   Pan - mun - jom,
5. Bud - dy Hol - ly, Ben Hur,   Space Mon - key, Ma - fi - a,

Bran - do, The King and I, and The Catch - er in the Rye.
Hu - la - hoops, Cas - tro, Ed - sel is a no go.

Ei - sen - how - er, vac - cine, Eng - land's got a new queen,
U - 2, Syng - man Rhee, pay - o - la and Ken - ne - dy.

Mar - ci - a - no, Li - ber - a - ce, San - ta - ya - na good - bye.)
Chub - by Check - er, Psy - cho, Bel - gians in the Con - go.)

Chorus

We did - n't start the fi - re. It was al - ways burn - ing since the

world's been turn - ing. We did - n't start the fi - re. No, we

did - n't light ___ it, but we tried to fight ___ it.

Verse

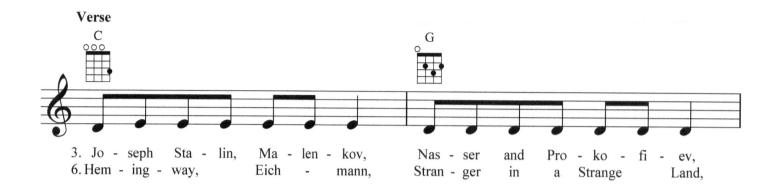

3. Jo - seph Sta - lin, Ma - len - kov, Nas - ser and Pro - ko - fi - ev,
6. Hem - ing - way, Eich - mann, Stran - ger in a Strange Land,

Rock - e - fel - ler, Cam - pa - nel - la, Com - mu - nist Bloc.
Dy - lan, Ber - lin, Bay of Pigs In - va - sion.

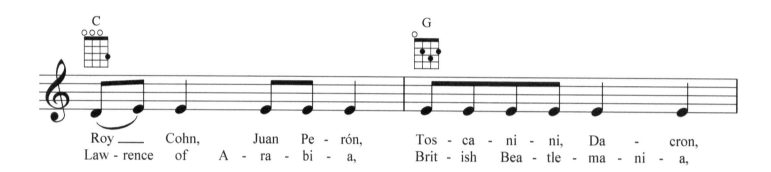

Roy ___ Cohn, Juan Pe - rón, Tos - ca - ni - ni, Da - cron,
Law - rence of A - ra - bi - a, Brit - ish Bea - tle - ma - ni - a,

Dien Bien Phu falls, "Rock A - round the Clock."
Ole Miss, John Glenn, Lis - ton beats Pat - ter - son.

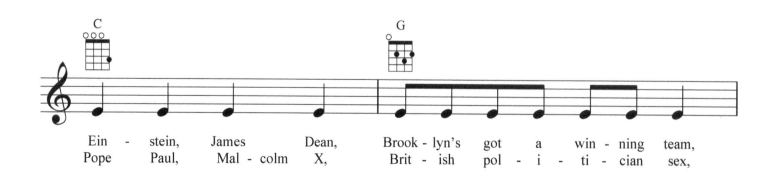

Ein - stein, James Dean, Brook - lyn's got a win - ning team,
Pope Paul, Mal - colm X, Brit - ish pol - i - ti - cian sex,

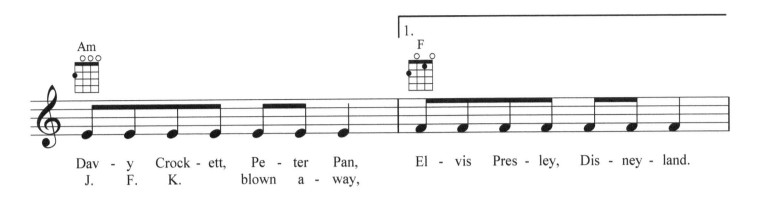

Dav - y Crock - ett, Pe - ter Pan, El - vis Pres - ley, Dis - ney - land.
J. F. K. blown a - way,

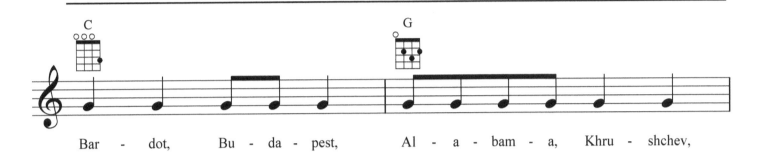

Bar - dot, Bu - da - pest, Al - a - bam - a, Khru - shchev,

Chorus

Prin - cess Grace, Pey - ton Place, trou - ble in the Su - ez. We did - n't start the fi -

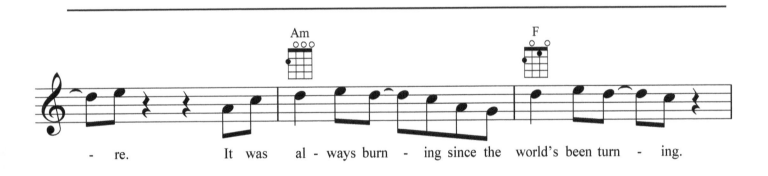

- re. It was al - ways burn - ing since the world's been turn - ing.

We did - n't start the fi - re. No, we did - n't light __ it, but we

tried to fight __ it. 4. Lit - tle Rock, Pas - ter - nak, Mic - key Man - tle, Ker - ou - ac,

Sput - nik, Chou En - Lai, Bridge on the Riv - er Kwai. Leb - a - non, Charles de Gaulle,

Cal - i - for - nia base - ball, Stark - weath - er, hom - i - cide, chil - dren of Tha - lid - o - mide.

what else do I have to say? We did - n't start the fi -

- re. It was al - ways burn - ing since the world's been turn - ing.

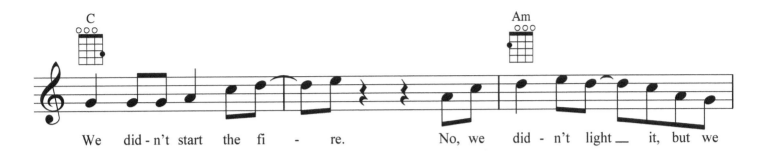

We did-n't start the fi - re. No, we did - n't light __ it, but we

Verse

tried to fight __ it. 7. Birth con-trol, Ho Chi Minh, Rich-ard Nix-on back a - gain.

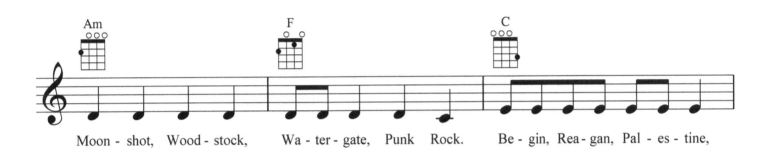

Moon - shot, Wood - stock, Wa - ter - gate, Punk Rock. Be - gin, Rea - gan, Pal - es - tine,

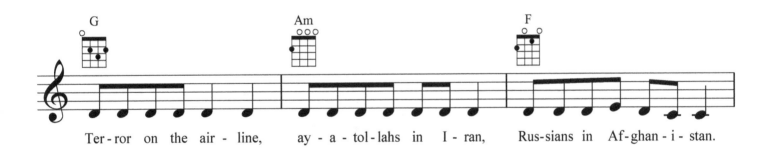

Ter - ror on the air - line, ay - a - tol - lahs in I - ran, Rus - sians in Af - ghan - i - stan.

Wheel of For - tune, Sal - ly Ride, heav - y met - al, su - i - cide, for - eign debts, home - less vets,

AIDS, crack, Ber - nie Goetz. Hy - po - der-mics on the shore, Chi-na's un - der mar-tial law,

Outro-Chorus

Rock and Roll- er, Co - la Wars, I can't take it an - y - more. We did - n't start the fi -

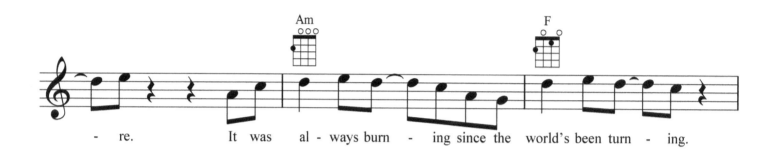

- re. It was al - ways burn - ing since the world's been turn - ing.

We did - n't start the fi - re. But when we are gone, __ will it

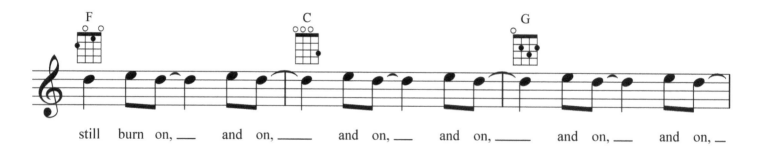

still burn on, __ and on, ____ and on, __ and on, ____ and on, __ and on, __

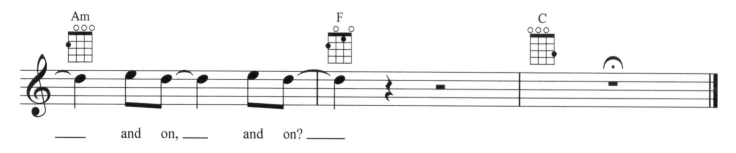

____ and on, ___ and on? ____

Y.M.C.A.

Words and Music by Jacques Morali, Henri Belolo and Victor Willis

young man,   pick your - self off the   ground. __   I said,
young man,   when you're short on your   dough. __   You can

young man,   'cause you're in a new town __   there's no
stay there   and I'm sure you will find __   man - y

1., 3., 5.   2., 4., 6.

need to __   be _____ un - hap - py.
ways to __   have __   __ a good time.

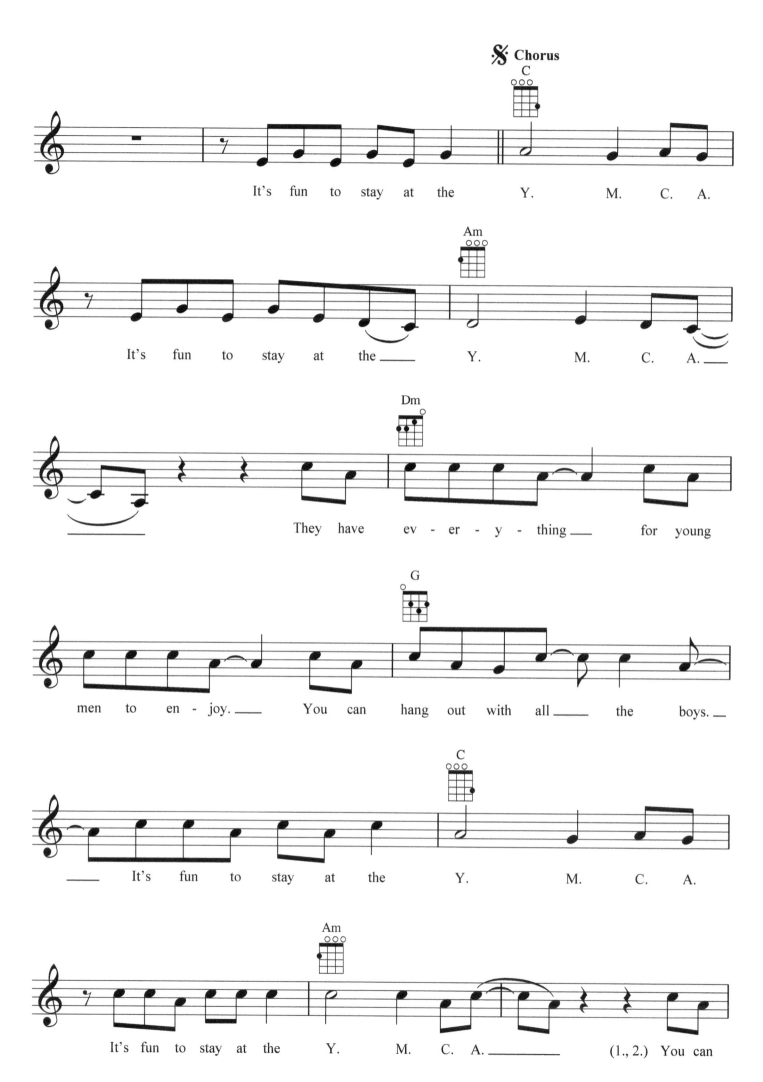

get your-self clean, ___ you can have a good meal. ___ You can
(3., 4.) Young man, young man, ___ { there's no need to feel down. ___ }
{ are you lis-t'ning to me? ___ }

do what-ev-er ___ you feel. ___
Young man, young man, { pick your- }
{ what do }

1., 2.
D.C.
(with repeat)

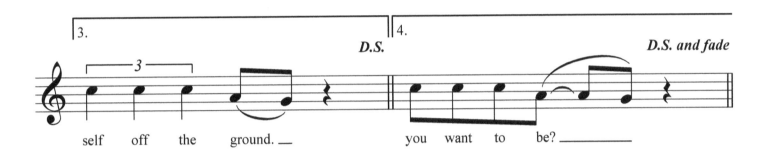

3.
self off the ground. ___

4.
D.S.
you want to be? ___
D.S. and fade

Additional Lyrics

3. Young man, are you listening to me?
   I said, young man, what do you want to be?
   I said, young man, you can make real your dreams
   But you've got to know this one thing:

4. No man does it all by himself.
   I said, young man, put your pride on the shelf
   And just go there to the Y.M.C.A.
   I'm sure they can help you today.

5. Young man, I was once in your shoes.
   I said, I was down and out and with the blues.
   I felt no man cared if I were alive.
   I felt the whole world was so jive.

6. That's when someone came up to me
   And said, "Young man, take a walk up the street.
   It's a place there called the Y.M.C.A.
   They can start you back on your way."

Where Have All the Flowers Gone?

Words and Music by Pete Seeger

First note

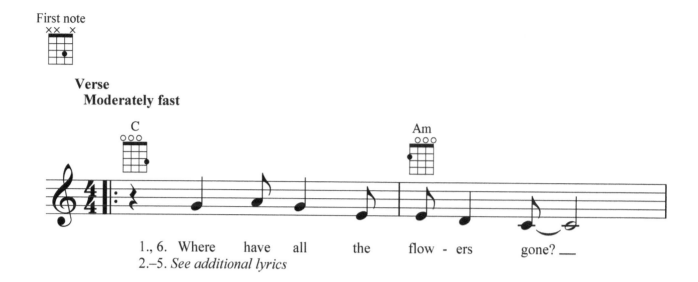

Verse
Moderately fast

1., 6. Where have all the flow - ers gone? ___
2.–5. *See additional lyrics*

Long time pass - ing. ___ Where have all the

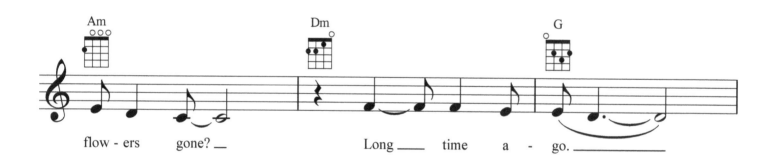

flow - ers gone? ___ Long ___ time a - go. ___

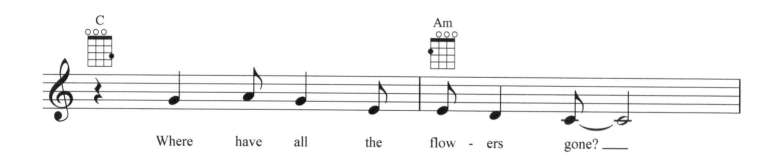

Where have all the flow - ers gone? ___

Young girls ___ have picked them, ev - 'ry one. ___

Oh, when will ___ they ev - er learn? Oh, when will

they ev - er learn? ___

learn? ___

Additional Lyrics

2. Where have all the young girls gone?
Long time passing.
Where have all the young girls gone?
Long time ago.
Where have all the young girls gone?
Gone for husbands, every one.
Oh, when will they ever learn?
Oh, when will they ever learn?

3. Where have all the husbands gone?
Long time passing.
Where have all the husbands gone?
Long time ago.
Where have all the husbands gone?
Gone for soldiers, every one.
Oh, when will they ever learn?
Oh, when will they ever learn?

4. Where have all the soldiers gone?
Long time passing.
Where have all the soldiers gone?
Long time ago.
Where have all the soldiers gone?
Gone to graveyards, every one.
Oh, when will they ever learn?
Oh, when will they ever learn?

5. Where have all the graveyards gone?
Long time passing.
Where have all the graveyards gone?
Long time ago.
Where have all the graveyards gone?
Gone to flowers, every one.
Oh, when will they ever learn?
Oh, when will they ever learn?

Who'll Stop the Rain

Words and Music by John Fogerty

First note

Verse
Moderately

1. Long   as   I _____   re - mem - ber,   the
2. I   went   down ___ Vir - gin - ia   seek - ing
3. Heard   the   sing - ers   play - ing;

rain _____   been   com - in'   down, _____
shel - ter   from   the   storm. _____
how _____   we   cheered   for   more. _____   The

clouds   of   mys - t'ry   pour - in'   con -
Caught   up   in _____   the   fa - ble,   I
crowd   had   rushed ___ to - geth - er,

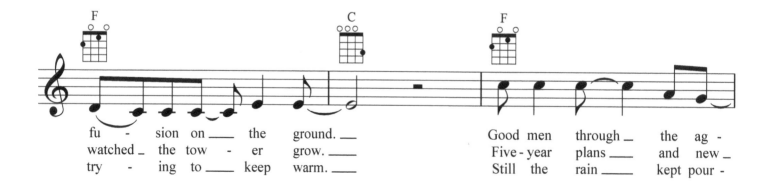

fu - sion   on ___ the   ground. ___   Good   men   through ___ the   ag -
watched ___ the   tow - er   grow. ___   Five - year   plans ___ and   new ___
try - ing   to ___ keep   warm. ___   Still   the   rain _____ kept   pour -

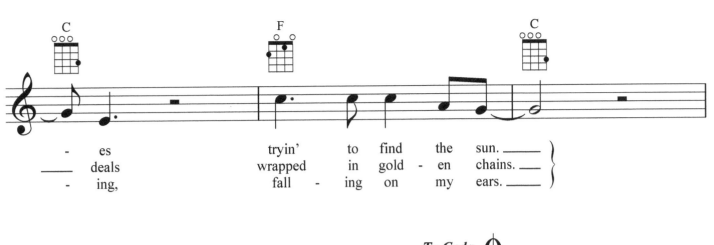

- es
____ deals
- ing,

tryin'   to   find   the   sun. _____
wrapped   in   gold - en   chains. __
fall - ing   on   my   ears. _____

To Coda ✛

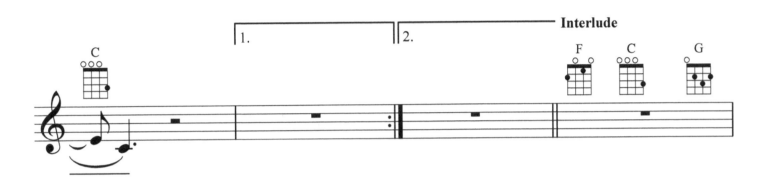

And I won - der,   still I won - der: who'll   stop   the   rain? __

Interlude

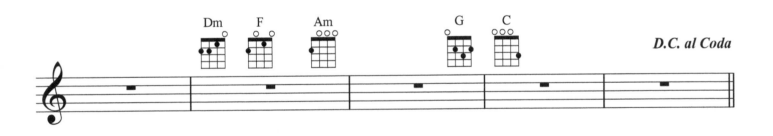

D.C. al Coda

✛ **Coda**

who'll   stop   the   rain? _____

Why Walk When You Can Fly

Words and Music by Mary Chapin Carpenter

Interlude (Outro)

walk   when   you ___ can   fly?

Additional Lyrics

2. In this world there's a whole lot of sorrow,
   In this world there's a whole lot of shame.
   In this world there's a whole lot of sorrow and a whole lot of ground to gain.

Chorus: When you spend your whole life wishing, wanting and wondering why,
   It's a long enough life to be living; why walk when you can fly?

3. In this world there's a whole lot of golden,
   In this world there's a whole lot of plain.
   In this world you've a soul for a compass and a heart for a pair of wings.

Chorus: There's a star on the far horizon, rising bright in an azure sky.
   For the rest of the time that you're given, why walk when you can fly?

Wonder

Words and Music by Natalie Merchant

First note

Verse
Moderately

C   G   Am   G

1. Doc - tors ___ have ___ come ___ from dis - tant cit -
2. News - pa - pers ___ ask ___ in - ti - mate ques -

F   C   G

- ies   just to see ___ me,   stand o - ver my bed, ___
- tions,   want con - fes - sions,   reach in - to my head ___

Am   G   F

___   dis - be - liev - ing   what they're see - ing. }
___ to   steal the glo - ry   of my sto - ry. } They say I ___

Chorus

C   G   Am   G   F

___ must be one ___ of the won - ders of God's own cre - a - tion.

C   G   Am   G

(1., 2.) And as far ___ as they see, ___ they can of - fer no ___ ex - pla - na -
(3.) And as far ___ as you see, ___ you can of - fer me no ex - pla - na -

To Coda

- ed.
- fer.

With love, with pa - tience and _____ with faith, _____

she'll make her way, _____

she'll make her way." _____

Verse

3. Peo - ple ___ see ___ me; ___

I'm a chal - lenge to your bal - ance.

I'm o - ver your heads; ___ how I con - found ___

Yellow Submarine

Words and Music by John Lennon and Paul McCartney

The Wind Beneath My Wings

from the Original Motion Picture BEACHES

Words and Music by Larry Henley and Jeff Silbar

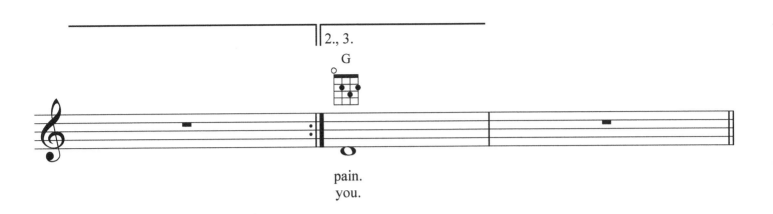

pain.
you.

2., 3.

𝄋 **Chorus**

Did you ev - er know ____ that you're my he - ro
Did you ev - er know ____ that you're my he - ro?

and ev - 'ry - thing I _____ would like to
You're ev - 'ry - thing I _____ wish I could

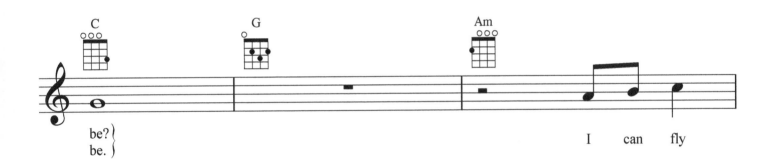

be?
be.

I can fly

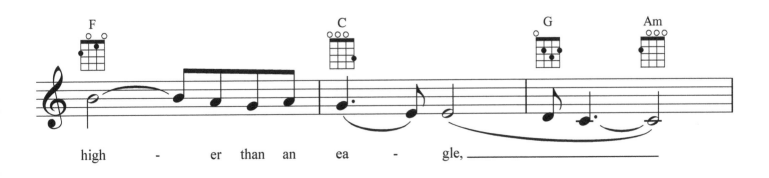

high - er than an ea - gle, _____

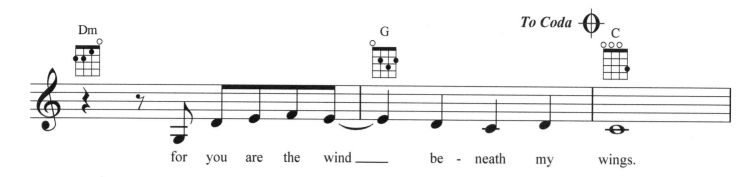

for you are the wind _____ be - neath my wings.

D.C. al Coda
(take 2nd ending)

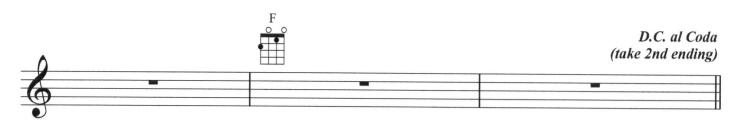

Coda

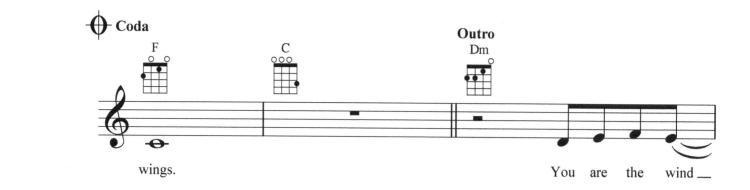

wings.

Outro

You are the wind __

be - neath my wings. _____

Additional Lyrics

2. So I was the one with all the glory,
   While you were the one with all the strength.
   A beautiful face without a name for so long,
   A beautiful smile to hide the pain.

3. It might have appeared to go unnoticed,
   But I've got it all here in my heart.
   I want you to know I know the truth, of course I know it.
   I would be nothing without you.